Double Chocolate
a book of exotic love

Forget love - I'd rather fall in chocolate.

~ Sandra J. Dykes

Double Chocolate
a book of exotic love

Suzanne Deakins

Cover Design by William Floyd

Interior design and layout
One Spirit Press, LLC
Portland, Oregon

One Spirit Press, LLC
Portland, Oregon 97214
OneSpiritpress@gmail.com

dedicated

dedicated to God
the only source of love
to my lovers
to all who want to know love
to all who have loved
to all who have been loved

and in memory of Tim Dickey

Chocolate is madness it is delight.

~Judith Olney

thank you

First to my children, Gregg, Stephen, Michael, Gabriella, Andrew and Ethan... for more than anyone they taught me about love.

To Catherine Wilkerson who gave me my grandson, Eildon Gabriel.

To Billye Talmadge whom I have loved from the first moment I met her. She helped to set me free so I could come from behind that glass wall and have voice.

To my brother Bill Floyd for a wonderful piece of art for the cover and the cover design.

To Randy Rencsok because you exist and are loved.

To Greg Fiendell, whom I have never met, but he guided me to a less abstract way of thinking about poetry.

To P.M.H. for reading and commenting on my work with intelligence and insight into language.

To (Andy) Andrew J, Manché who so loves love that I could not help but think of his consciousness when I wrote.

To Acara because you are love personified and a true sister.

To Derek Lamar because you hated it and loved it.

To Aaron Yeagle because you asked me to post.

To David Kohl for your support.

And to Mary Spiers-Floyd for her chocolate recipes.

table of contents

Soft Kisses...101

The Dawn of Consciousness...133

Chocolate, Chocolate, Chocolate

Colophon...240

About Love

No matter where you travel in the world you will find people interested in love, being loved, loving, obsessed by love and desire. The very act of loving is healthy for our bodies and minds. And of course chocolate imitates some of the emotions of love and acts similarly in our bodies as does love.

Love sometimes comes in the form of obsession wanting to posses the object of love, to control it. It often comes with pain of knowing it won't last and of course it comes with desire. Desire is often mistaken for love, the physical desire of sexual encounter. There are many aspects of love and many attributes. I have not been able to cover all of them. There are many different kinds of love such as absolute love. One thing I am sure of is that love is an act of higher mind, God, conscious awareness, and divine source.

For me it is better to have loved intensely for a short period of time rather than not have had love at all. I have grown to know that I can love many and that once I have been loved or have loved that those bonds of love can never be broken. Even in the most torrid of love affairs that crash and burn, love does not cease.

In love we desire to be known and penetrated in such a way that our souls and desires are naked before our lover. In loving we want to feel safe. To feel safe enough so that what we call real can be known and not threatened. The romance of those moments is simply this desire to understand that we are safe, and not alone ... we seek to break through the isolation that is so painful.

I am not sure what being-in-love means to you. I have thought about it and wondered if it is something different than just loving. Is there some magic in being-in-love that is different than just loving? Is there a level of intimacy, a level of commitment to the beloved? There is definitely a chemistry between people that turns them into lovers or lanquishing in pain of the unfulfilled. There are also those very loving relationships that grow over time without chemistry until later on in life. Whatever being-in-love means it seems illusive to me today… perhaps tomorrow I will better understand it.

It saddens me to think we teach nothing of loving and intimacy in our schools and churches. In America and most of the Western world we hide behind Victorian morals that have long ago proved to be harmful to our psychological wellbeing. Love and all that comes with it between consenting adults is beautiful and I believe is sanctioned by God. And is in fact an act of knowing God. All life is created out of love no matter what the seeming circumstance… child, soup, or art are all acts of love. All of which are beloved to the creator or source of life.

All of this brings me to say. I hope you are being loved and loving. Enjoy these poems, find meaning and yourself in a few of them… experience the pain in some… read them to your beloved. Dwell in the state of ecstasy finding love in all aspects of your life.

July 3, 2008
West Linn, Oregon

Chocolate, of course, is the stuff of which fantasies are made. Rich, dark, velvety-smooth fantasies that envelop the senses and stir the passions.

~Judith Olney

Passion

Passion and desire drive us to do many things. I am passionate about existence, consciousness, and love. I believe that great stores of energy are released when I allow my passions and desires out of their boxes and into my life. I don't want milquetoast love, I want passion and to be wanted passionately... This section is about those moments of passion ... those words most of us long to hear.

Double Chocolate

Dark chocolate, dark and silky not too sweet
darkness covering me
I am beckoned into pulsating dark

Swirling, misting covering me in secrets
Softness against softness
Silk against silk

Pulsating dark twists and turns
Throbbing in its desire to remain secret
Silk against silk

Darkness pushing gently to enter me
Secret of all secrets
Wants of all wants
How can I avoid this
Pushing gently to enter me

Surrendering to the darkness
Feeling the softness of silk
Surrendering to the secrets
Knowing the wanting

Tongue twisting and tasting
Desire with out fulfillment
Sensual smell of the sweetness

Reaching to touch
Reaching through the dark to find you
Melting in the heat of dark
Throbbing
Wanting
Desiring

The passion of Double Chocolate

November 1, 2007

Branded Flesh

Blank pages left unstained and ink without use…
for days I have waited for your letter,
your note to tell me you loved me and wanted me.
I know you love me… say it… sing it to me, write it to me.

How am I to make you mine?
Do I dare ask to touch you?
For one moment of your voice saying
those most sacred words
I would sell my soul… drink poison.

I see you in the distance
Dancing with others
Touching others
But you leave me laying waiting for you

Harlot, slut, whore… you give my love to another
Leaving me naked in the hot sands
My disguise ripped and
my last mask falling from my face

I see your beauty reflecting off the mirror
Your image has been branded into my naked flesh
Raw flesh begging you to say it…

You have branded me for life…
Fleshy love begging you to say it
Ink stained fingers longing to hold you

Branded for life… if you will not take me
Who will want this flesh you have left…
Say it, say it… I know you love me

Take my flesh write on it…
Burn the words I would die for in it.
Say it , say it… write it in my flesh

November 6, 2007

24 Hours

I have throbbed and paced in wanting you
Nothing ceases this passion and desire
Wind blows, leaves fall
and winter peeks through my windows

For 24 hours I waited for you in my heart

Hoping beyond hope you would appear
I find myself raging and in stillness in this passion
Naked, my heart is without safety it awaits you
I still want you

Come to me… do not make me ache so much
Dance with me in the stars
Soar with me to our dreams
I want you

Find me in my pain and desire to know you
Reach through the mist of our dream
Touch me… give me reality
Want me

For 24 hours I waited for you in my heart

Scrape the ice from my window so I may see you coming
Rake the leaves so I may see your footprint upon my grass
Knock gently upon my door
for it stands ready to open to you
I am waiting

Climb in my bed beside me
Touch me so I may once more know the warmth
Kiss me so I may breath again
give me life once more

Whisper to me of our love so I may again hear
Be with me in the pain and pleasure
so I may know our wholeness
Wrap me in your love
take me to the stars
so we may be
I want you

Sit with me in my heart

November 5, 2007

Entrance Strategies

I knew you were coming
But not when
I knew it would be you
knocking at my door

You arrived at midnight
Your entrance into my life was not planned
how can I describe what has happened
you have thrown my fear away

You did not tell me you were coming at this hour
I had not planned that you would be in my life
I opened the door naked and
unprepared for your appearance
you have stripped me of my masks

You wanted me to tell you what it felt like
But I cannot,
how am I to tell you of my nakedness,
of the me that no longer exists

You should have told me the hour
I would have prepared for you
instead I stand without a place to hide
I can no longer be without your love

You wanted to love me at midnight
How could I not love you
You have ripped the pretenses from my body
you have known all of me

I had not planned for you in my life
you came in my side door
I would have planned your entrance
prepared my heart for you

You have come into my life
taken my secrets
exposed them to your love
how does one prepare for this?

Don't tell me it is forever
I have not prepared
give me this one moment
let me open the door to my heart

November 20, 2007

Love In The Morning

I can feel your soft buttocks against my stomach
and the fleshy love we will enjoy swells within me.
The scent of your body fills my nose.
I reach to draw you closer to me
in this one delicious moment.
I want you in my arms.

Breathing upon your shoulder
I find myself in one instance of love with you.
Small beads of sweat on your body fill the air
with the scent of your being

Our eyes meet for an eternity as our
lips reach for each other.
Bolts of fire run through my body
as our love cascades toward a new place.

I feel my surrender to you
as we walk a path no other has known.
I descend deeper into your being
exploring the very core of existence and
am sent to new realizations of love.

Breathless we reach for a moment of immortality…
ascending in a crescendo as our beings merge.
I will know all of you…
in this one moment of love.

And for the first time you will know me... all of me...
Our path is clear the love of being
has taken us to unforetold places in life.

We could have missed this moment in life past...
this exquisite moment so full of love.
The song within is so strong
it will drown out all previous music of love...

I will know you for an eternity.
We will know the heaven and hell, the god within.
Once more our bodies touch
and our sweat combines in the
symbolic ritual of our merging...

Our scent is no longer individual but the scent of two
becoming one in a morning of love.
Our love scent, beyond all comprehension,
fills me with such tranquility and craving...
known only to the tides and stars.

Opening my eyes to the morning light
I see your empty pillow.
The mist of my dream rolls back
revealing another morning without you in my bed.

Soft tears fall on my pillow
your scent no longer clings to me.
Once again my prayer has gone unfulfilled.
I want you in my bed, in my dream, in my arms.

October 2007

I Would Have You In My Bed

When I woke this morning
I stretched… snuggled down
Pulled my comforter over my head
Only 6 days left until you will share my bed

Silly things going through my mind
Thinking about all we have said,
all we have not said.
Wanting my fingers to comb through your hair.

Imagining we are kissing,
I can feel your tongue
My lips tingle with the feel of you
Lips sucking the very breath of me.

My body is on fire this morning
Everything that touches me
reminds me of you
my hand imagines what your
buttocks will feel like.

Turning over dreaming of
the feel of your hair
along my legs and back.
Pulling you to me with your hair

Tasting your neck
Smelling your chest
Kissing you deeply
An eternity spent kissing your velvet lips

Small moans
rolling around in my bed
heat in my throat
throbbing in my wanting of you

If you were here,
I would devour you
Taste you and have all of you
6 days until I will have you in my bed.

December 16, 2007

Obsession

I woke this morning wanting you
Obsessed with wanting you
tied to my heart
How am I to be free of you?

You came into my life
but did not tell me the price
I would pay
obsessed by my needing of you.

Each time my mind whispers your name
my soul smolders in its wanting of you,
my heart pounds uncontrolled when
the thought of you comes to me.

The hands that would write
of my addiction
are on fire unable to hold my pen
the paper scorched from the heat

You did not tell me our first kiss
would addict me to you…
like a poison your kiss infected
my very being.

Standing in the hot shower
waiting for the water
to wash your bond away
take this obsession from me.

Free me from this poison
take it from me
let me breathe again
let me know life without you.

This love has left me twisted and tied to you
in human bondage, alone and joined
addicted unable to let go
pulled deeper each day into you

Obsessed by my love for you
what good would I be without you
withering and dying
needing the very poison that keeps me

Obsessed by your love
Held in human bondage
for all time
Don't take your poison from me

Take my smoldering soul
twist my heart
let my fingers burn
in their wanting to touch you
Do not take your love from me

let me have my obsession
let the poison remain
bind me to you for an eternity

January 20, 2008

Darkness Beckons

Evil beckons to us this night,
dark love,
secret loves
love without purpose

Tormented by unsatisfied desires
feverish in its wanting
seeking to know the pain of pleasure
desiring the burning

Darkness calls us
into chasms of no return
hellish screams
dark dreams

Across the veil of darkness
into the land of evil
no light exists
only that which would imprison

Wickedness hides in every corner
luring us further into unexplored
places of gloom
nothing can cleanse these moments

Beauty lost in timeless shadows
peace hidden beneath the screams
flesh on fire
thrusting into realms of eternity
pain becomes ecstasy

January 20 2008

Reaching

Reaching, touching
feeling the velvet space between
Starlight flooding our eyes.

Reaching touching
feeling the fire that burns within
moonlight washing over our face

Reaching touching
feeling the waves within
sunlight warming our skin

Reaching touching
passion ever present
essence flooding our nose

Reaching touching
finding you in my life
being knowing being

October 20, 2007

I'll Never Stop Loving You

I'll never stop loving you
the moon will stop shining
the stars will leave the sky
before I stop loving you

I 'll never stop loving you
The world will stop turning
The seas stop being
and time will stand still

Before I stop loving you
day will turn to night
and the birds will stop singing
life would not be

I'll never stop loving you
no matter what you say
no matter how it is
you can't make me stop loving you

Before I stop loving you
the sun will stop shining
the clouds stop whispering
the sands will turn cold

You can turn from me
try to forget me
stop saying my name
but you cant make me stop loving you

Even if you leave me
and take away my heart
imprison my soul
I'll never stop loving you

If I stopped loving you
my life has no purpose
my soul has no existence
life would not be

You cannot make me stop loving you.

January 28, 2008

Passion With a Stranger

I want to be the first one you look for
when you come into a room.
If we kiss I want you to respond
with a kiss full of desire

Be passionate for me
be full of desire
your skin is sumptuously soft
your sex is what I want

Such selfish pleasure
can only be had with a stranger
delightful tastes and smells
no attachment, no future

We are lovers and
cannot stop
with the pleasure that
brings screams in the middle of the
afternoon

Time and circumstance
will take me away from your body
I will feel cold when you are gone
my flesh will not burn

Such a selfish pleasure
with the stranger you are
no ties to dictate the course of love
no emotion to hold back the passion

Love is dangerous to those
who would seek it
with a stranger
there are no rules with strangers

We who have sought
passion with strangers
find ourselves in a world
filled with fantasy

No rules
no predicated course of action
only passion in fantasy
love in imagination

Our bodies aflame with desire
knowing that these moments
may be all that we ever have
star filled moments of passion.

There are no rules with strangers

February 18, 2008

How Am I to Know

I come here waiting for you.
wanting you to come
desiring to see you
to see your words

Hours I have pursued you
waiting, not breathing
just waiting
blurry eyes lingering in the darkness
music blaring to lock out the quiet

I come here every night
waiting for you to appear
yearning to see you
one more time

Stretching hands out to touch you
finding nothing to feel
tears falling upon my shirt.
One more time, please one more time

Every night I wait for you
I do not breathe when I come
afraid that my very breath
will drive you away.

What kind of hell
have we created with our love?
What kind of torture it is not to know?
Will we have the courage
to call, to hear...

This fantasy makes me mad
with desire for you.
my imagination finds you in my life
heart pounding wildly with longing

How am I to know?
Are you real?
Or is this a game
I have thought up
in my loneliness

Chat with me one more time!

December 13, 2007

Malignancy

I draw my strength from this malignancy
Seeped in my own blood and sweat.
The blood soiling my body,
sweat stinging my eyes.

Reaching through the netting
you cease to exist
a reason to be ashamed
a reason to hide.

This is a malignancy we share
finding our strength in that which we abhor.
Tempered walls and windows facing the street
midday noises stir my fear.

Touching your soft sex
stroking your skin
this malignancy we share
strengthens my resolve to let you go.

This love is so strong
it will never be again in a lifetime.
My soul should know this
but the malignancy is too great

We will be parted
not allowed to live in what we abhor and love.
Endless lifetime of endless sands
stretch before me.

Void where life never had a chance
Ink stains upon paper
my only companion
grey world of the malignancy

Say it to me one last time
Say it for me one first time
Tell me you abhor what we are.

January 22, 2008

Soar With Me

Is this the dream I have been dreaming?
Is this living the dream that is dreamt?
Where are you in my dream?

Where are my wings,
today I will soar.
to fly above the dream to
be everywhere at once.

Standing on the chasm of insanity
I want to leap over...
into the experience most feared,
wanting to know love.

Standing on this ledge of all time
peering below, but all there is to see
and hear is chaos.
Insanity screaming words without meaning.
Is there love in this chaos?

Are you hiding there from me?
Struggling to awake, the dream will not end...
Where are you?
Is our existence in this insanity?

Slowly turning from the cliff of chaos
my wings are unfolding
searching for the direction of the stars,
in this moment I will know love...

You will be found
And we will know ourself as one.
no longer be alone...
locked in solitary confinement.

Slowly reaching for you
taking you to me so we may fly
in this one everlasting moment.

Knowing love takes us beyond the dream
soaring among the stars
our hearts swell

If this is reality or if it is a dream
please let it never stop.
Come unfold your wings and soar
with me to the center of all ...
be with me in love.

November 5, 2007

When I Left

When I left
your scent clung to me
my hair and body

All night long
you lingered
hovering in my mind
stirring my senses

Your scent clung to me
in every pore of my being
I could sense your existence
like fingers reaching through the veil

You found me in the dark
swirling your scent arousing me
creating new passion
as the moon shone through the window

Your scent awakens me
to imaginings yet untold
like a magic potion
you bind me to you

The first stirring of dawn
brings you nearer
spilling into my being
your potions of love

Every pore of my being
holds your life
your scent of existence   *April 22, 2008*

You Filled My Night

I went to bed and you were there on my mind
tossing and turning thinking of you,
imagining what it would be like to have you beside me
touching me, wanting me

Through the night your image filled my dreams
stormy love and passion untold romps through my head
in my dreams I reach out to touch you
dreaming of your touch and love on me

Wanting you in my bed this morning
I am filled with passion
and the need to love you
rolling over on my back I wonder

How will you fit into my life?
What if you leave me?

Come to me in my dream
or in my day time
but come and be with me
let me know and love you

How am I to survive this passion I feel for you?

November 23, 2007

Lover Come To Me

I look into your eyes
and recognize something familiar
the intensity is too great
my head turns from you.

Your soul is gleaming in your eyes.
This is what I see in you
through our veil of existence.
Moving our veil aside
I will behold your entirety.

Come to me my lover
let me know you
lift your veil so I may
look upon the beauty
beholding your very soul.

Lay naked next to me
let me know your heart
feel the warmth of being
I would see your flesh

Come to me my lover
give me of your desire
reach through my veil
discover who I am

Touch my body with your love
come to my core of being.
Let no part of my being go
untouched by your love

Come to me my lover
lets us know each other.
Make love with me my lover
passionate wanting
desiring totality
giving all

Throw your masks into the ocean
burn your veils
be naked with me on the sands of time.

Come to me my lover.

December 15, 2007

Naked and Unadorned

Into my life you came
naked and unadorned
standing before me
without purpose of being.

Into my life you came
humble and wanting
unprotected soul
revealed for all to see

Encountering the phoenix
enduring the fire
cleansed of past darkness and
accepting new light.

Slowly taking your hand
leading you to my inner thoughts
into my life you have come.
naked and unadorned.

Rooms filled with life
air infused with spice
light filtered through bamboo
clouds running from the sun.

Down covers pulled over
soft whispers
gentle strokes
no more tears

Into my life you come
naked and open to be known
sleeping beside me
touching my body with your warmth.

I dropped my pretense
left my disguises behind
let me into your life
naked and unadorned

Enter into my being
naked and unadorned
become one in our life
moving to rhythm of the stars.

I come into your life
naked and unadorned.

December 30, 2007

My Woman

Sensual strength
Blond, brown, or black
Deliberate elegance, flawless
Perfection of god in motion

Body moving to the rhythm
Of all time and space
Sexy, sultry, feminine, grooving to life
A gentle breeze riding the waves of light

Lighting the room with radiance of being
Calming the rough seas of life
Lucid beauty
Intelligence walking symphony

My woman, every women
The priestess of life
Smiling, full of grace and style
Never underdone

My woman, every women
Its not just the flow of her hair
Or the power of her stare
There is no other woman but my woman

Confidence in her walk
The ring in her voice
Curve of her hips
The point of her lips

That makes her all women
Gods greatest creation
Opening to me with a twist
Exotic, erotically packaged
Sealed with a kiss

My woman all woman

for Billye
April 15, 2008

Setting Love Free

Beloved,

Today we went over a threshold,
a place I have never gone with another
Perhaps this place has only been visited
with my words,
but maybe not even then
You will have to take the lead
I am not sure I can

You have entered every part of me
filled me
and allowed me to flow into you
I suspect this is the motion of love
conceivably this is what happens
when love is set free

I am glad we waited
until today to go here.
You have all of me
in our coming together
my will is surrendered to what will be

I am not sure of purpose
other than
it could never be satisfied by sex alone.
This passion goes beyond body, mind, and soul...
Perhaps this place is more than sacred
it is a sanctuary for love and compassion...

I will have all of you
I want all of you
every atom,
molecule, cell
your thoughts,
tears
laughter

I want to explore it all
breathing it into my being.
passing into you
seeing you from the inside out...
I want you to be with me...

Devour me in love
desire and passion...
No words can describe
ardor and craving
I feel for you tonight

I can't write more
because I simply can't explain it,
or describe it...
perhaps it is God, I don't know
we have set love free

Spetember 30, 2007

The Day of Birth and Death

This mist is lifting from my mind,
lifting my thoughts
to mountains and tree tops
moonlight beckons
the sunlight
shadows begin to wane

The rarity of air produces a sound
a slight tingle fills my being
I have never walked to this place before
never seen these trees.
The tree that is mine must be found today
this is to be the day of death and birth.

The mist is lifting from my mind,
taking my thoughts to the mountains
and to the depths of the oceans.
moonlight embraces the shadows.

Filling my being with sound of life
melting fear that would
hide in the shadows.
Ancients rise in me
bringing me this initiation.
Today is the day of death and birth

The mist is lifting from my mind,
carrying my thoughts to your lips
to your being...
Reaching to touch the lips that speak of love
and find them speaking..
You lift me
and in my mind a clarity and passion
Knowing not before this time

in this one moment you will take me
to the mountain and oceans

Death will be known
You permeate my being
shadows disappear
your lips speak of life
and light and
love of life.

My body finds the rhythm
of your body
it finds you are whole and perfect
in your love of life

The mist is lifting from my mind,
my thoughts go to God.
as you penetrate my being
a passion never realized before
we will pass through the head of God
and be born again

The passion of two has
become the fire of one,
consuming the mist and
fear that would destroy love

My hand gently reaches to know all of you
all of the shadows,
cracks and secrets
Consciousness can not hide
from Consciousness this day.

Today is to be the day of death and birth

September 26, 2007

Lust

Every night for a month
I have come to this park,
waiting for a small glimpse of you.
I know you see me
I can feel you looking at me.
Why do you hide in this way?
Reach out and take my hand…
trust me.

I see that heart you wear
on your sleeve and
the tear in your eyes…
you are tired and afraid,
but why do you hide from me?
Let me touch you…
please let me touch you.

Should I want you less,
feel less lustful toward you?
How can we continue this way
in such pain
so cloaked in our lust
fearing it will escape…
How am I to know you
if you will not trust me?

Your beauty glows in my mind
fills my sight.
How can you not allow me
to know you in this way?

You stand naked before me,
wings curled around yourself.
If you let me touch your wings

for one small minute
we will soar.
Let my lust for you carry us
you can trust me.

For one small moment
to nestle into your chest...
to feel your breath on my neck...
and your whisper in my ear...
to touch your body glowing
in the dark of the night...
You must come out of hiding
let me know you...
you must trust me.

How can I survive
for one more night
in this lust and desire?
My loins ach
my desire is so great
I can barely move.

Let me hear your golden voice
just once.
Let me hear you say you
want me...
need me
must have me.

Wrap your wings around me
take me to you...
I am surrendered to your beauty
and our lust.

I trust you...   *November 7, 2007*

Sea of Sexuality

Come and swim with me
Swim with me in the sea
of sexuality

Drop your armor
Enter into this life naked
swim with me

Let your life flow
streams of sensuality
pouring into the sea of sexuality

Float upon the waves
Let them take you
And play upon their rhythm

Let go and be
Allowing the water
To kiss your body

Come and swim with me
In the sea of sexuality
Let the sea envelop you

Step into the pleasure
Bask in the desire
Be kissed by the sensual water

Dilate to meet
the maker of life
turn to see the waters

Come and swim with me
In the sea of sexuality
Let me taste the water of your life
Flow with the stream of
sensuality

Be naked and unafraid
Drop your armor
And swim with me

Let our lives meet
Upon the waves of the
Sea of sexuality

January 6, 2008

Chocolate is a divine, celestial drink, the sweat of the stars, the vital seed, divine nectar, the drink of the gods, panacea and universal medicine.

~ Geronimo Piperni, quoted by
Antonio Lavedán, Spanish army surgeon,1796

He felt now that he was not simply close to her, but that he did not know where he ended and she began.

~Leo Tokstoy

Sacred Love

Each moment spent in love is sacred. Every act of love, each time we make love, have an orgasm or just know we are loved we know the sacred a bit more... it is an act of God... higher mind, consciousness.

Our hopes and dreams as lovers are sacred. In love we are known, the consciousness our being is penetrated by another. We are searching for more than just a good time, but an intimate act of sharing and giving. Intimacy is not limited to bedroom. We reach to be intimate, to be accepted and wanted by another. To create a sacred space where none but the lover exists is our ultimate desire. Sacred love is an act of conscious awareness.

Make This My Prayer

Deep within me lies a need to be known by you.
I want you to want me, to love me,
to accept me.
This is my prayer
that you will know me and
find my soul for this one moment in all time.

Watch us as we go
and help us to be wise with one another,
to be kind and caring,
Let this be our prayer.

Guide us with grace,
let us find hope within our hearts for each other.
Let the stars we have watched
know that we are under the same sky.
Lead us to a place of safety within our hearts.

Let this be our prayer,
may we know the consciousness of love
and passion for our life.
May we share our dreams of life

Sharing the water of life
and the bread of being
let us this day form our covenant with Truth
Let us pray before the altar of all time
That we may be free of our enslavement

Teach us to light the candles of
Hope, peace, joy and love
So we may experience life everlasting
As one being loving one.

December 10, 2007

Suzanne Deakins

An Injunction from God

It was like an injunction from God
A command performance of love
And in the end our love was
lost in our story
like water in sand

Our story took all of our love
Diluting its very being
And we wept knowing
that we had not known
what we had was love

Through the years we waited
looking in the back of our mind
wanting to know and not asking
waves losing direction upon the shore

Music filling us up
Filling our senses through the years
Vanished moments of memory
floating over the ocean

Our love was an injunction from God
A command performance
Happening only once
A love never ending
A wanting never fulfilled

Lost in our story
obsessed by desire
vacant eyes finding nothing
hot empty sands
only my words to fill the void

An injunction from God to love   January 5 2008

Laying in Bed

Laying in bed,
smile on your lips as you sleep,
breezes blow in the window
bringing in the morning smells

Being licked by the flames of Ra
Glistening skin in the flames
How blessed this moment in time
to know this sacred space we share

I have spent a lifetime
waiting for this moment
embraced by the love I know
being licked by the flames of Ra

We could have missed this moment
Finding portals into our existence
Sacred spaces unexplored

January 1, 2008

Sensuality

The sensuality of life is God/Truth
beckoning us, seducing us, to stand in the absolute
in an orgasmic moment of ultimate sacred love.

An ultimate act in praise of the eternity of life
sex as anything less than this is illness,
an affliction
an error
and it should be burnt upon the altar
of the children yet unborn.

To see our self as gender ridden
choice laden
is to take the power of love
dash it against the darkness,
saying, "be-gone universe, you are no more."

That which is so cannot be chosen
nor can it be classified
Sensuality and sexuality are experiences
and have nothing to do with intellectual endeavors.

The intellect does not enter the promised land.
only the sensuality of God can take you to
that orgasmic moment known as life

So we desire, so shall it be

December 10, 2007

A Million Angels Sang Our Song

The light filled my heart
and the sound of the song
changed me for ever
we cannot return to the shadow

A million angels sang our song
filling our heart
a million stars shone in your eyes
and I gave you a million kisses deep

In this darkest time you
touched my soul
the song of the angels filled our heart

I did not try to understand
I only wanted to feel the
shinning of your lights

A million kisses deep
No place to hide
No path to run down

We only knew the light
and our touch
a million sunrises spent

One last kiss
sunrise
a million moons
and angels singing

August 2, 2009

Kiss Me

When the sunlight warms my soul
Kiss me and show me the way
Tell my grandfather to go
Turn me to the sun

I am on my way
To the place of sacred love
When the sunlight warms my soul
Kiss me

I dream of white crystals
I dream of stars
Tell my grandfather to go
Take me to the place of new birth

When the sunlight warms my soul
Kiss me and turn me to the south
Take me to the sanctified caves
Lead me to myself

Show me the way of my grandmother
Give me back my herbs
Give my will to the grandfather
Kiss me and take me to sacred love

As the night falls and my soul cools
Take me to the place of rain
Let me rest among the trees
Tell my grandmother to bring her herbs

As the moon rises in my life
Kiss me
Bring me to the place of new birth
Warm me with your love

Tell my grandfather to go
I am walking in my sleep
Wake me with your kiss
Don't let my soul grow cold

Let there be another day of sunlight
Warm my soul among my trees
Show me the eagle flying
Let me be on fire in my love

Grandmother bring your herbs
and show me the way
to the sanctified caves
where the mystery stays

Remember me as the child
of my grandmother
a child of the sun
a child of the stars

Remember me as the child
of the trees
kiss me and take me to sacred love
remember me in the moon

January 19, 2008

I Cannot Leave You

I will go where you go
Be where you will be
Love as you will love
For I can not leave you

Your bed shall be my bed
Your life my life
Your fortune mine
For I cannot leave you

I will walk with you
Reside in your house
Be by your side
For I can not leave you

My eyes will see you in the sun
My heart will great you from afar
My voice call your name when you are away
For I can not leave you

I will share my song with you
Grow our garden with you
Build a life with you
For I can not leave you

I will lay in your arms
And dream of angels
Watching the star they named for you
For I can not leave you

I will hold your hand
And swim in the ocean
Watching the sun set
For I can not leave you

And when our days are done
I will remain with you
I will love you without end
For I can not leave you

February 4, 2008

Breathing in Love

Tonight I remembered 1984
Living in the village in New York City
Walking along Christopher Street
Every time I go there my heart stops

Steve, David, Phil,
My love Constance,
Beloved Stephen and Gabriella
How many more names of death that year
I can barely breathe your names

Beautiful faces along the walk
Steps full of pain and sickness
Fear along every avenue
How will I remember to breathe

Your leaving took away my wanting to breathe
I would have gone in your place
I would have given my breath so that you may be
Beautiful faces that fade into the clouds of time

Who will remember to breathe your names
How soon will we forget those times
I let my balloons go to release you
Floating taking your worldly pain

Tell me how to breathe again
It does no good to hold you in sorrow
Yet if I release you what will be left?
Take my breath so you may be again

I am learning to breathe again
Holding my breath will do no good
For as time passes I can only remember
I remember my love for you

In the end I can only breathe in our love
And exhale our love.
What else can I offer you now
But a memory of love
With each breath I find my love for you

I can not give you my breath
I can only give you my memory of love
Breathing in all that was
Holding it in love
Breathing out new life of love

November 23, 2007

It Was Only a Poem

It was only a poem
No real meaning
A way of speaking so
no one would know

It was a way of saying
how I love you
telling you I care
and want you

It was only an ordinary
love poem
words that were secret
to us and our love

Our love is not known
too extraordinary to let out
Kept deep within our hearts
living only in our soul

A love the world has not known
Spoken only in a poem
known only to the soul
held in the hand of God

It was only a poem
But it gave me hope
It let my wings unfold
We can soar again

It was only a poem
but the words
changed my world
my soul took flight

Seeking to know you
Once more standing
above the head of God,
in all time

It was only a poem
but its words left me
in a prayer of thanksgiving
my splendor shining for all to see

Words of an incredible love
The very words reach out
Like loving hands
Touching my very being

It was only a poem but it changed my world.

for Derek
April 15, 2008

I Could Fall In Love With You

I could fall in love with you
I dream of your eyes
looking into mine
of your lips saying my name

I could fall in love with you
seeing you lay beside me
small sounds of breath
softness of being

I want you to fall in love with me
to dream of my eyes
looking into yours
of my lips saying your name

Taste us
Feel us
Our spirits mingle
Our laughter ripples through
all time

Rather ordinary people
with a simple life
walking and talking
holding hands
growing our garden

Laying in bed watching
spiders on the ceiling
shadows flickering

cats stretching
Ordinary people
with extraordinary love
uncomplicated feelings
simple existence

Timeless life
Spaceless knowing
of infinite thoughts of non-life
I want you to love me

Stroking our hair
Touching our flesh
Fingers desiring to know us

Say my name
say those sacred words
kiss my lips as I say it to you
let me kiss you as you say it to me

Ordinary plays of love
extraordinary existence of caring
look in my eyes
explore my soul
Let me sit in our soul
and take you to god
in my love for you take you
beyond all time and space

Take me to god
for this one eternal
moment of ecstasy
For it is whispered
we will be forever
for we exist as love

March 26, 2008

The Silence Fell

The silence fell
you could hear the mountain speak
a thousand years of silence
passed into the snow

The mountain answered us
you stood with your eyes closed
your heart open

The silence fell
the clouds sang
a hundred years of tears
flowed into the ocean

Tears floating
from closed eyes
love flowing
from open hearts

The silence fell
and your cry
of love was heard
sound witnessing love

Tear this silence from my lips
let my life be spoken
leave not the quiet
to speak of my being

The silence fell
and the lute could play
as the strings of my heart
were strummed by love

The song we are playing
is pure and full
the stars will dance
and the moon will sing

The silence fell
we could hear
as we closed our eyes
and opened our hearts.

Write our love in this song
Gently playing upon our hearts
Let the sound be

Close our eyes so we may feel.

January 11, 2008

Light Returns

Sons of Adam
Listen this day
hear ye my tongue

Sons of Adam
Come to the mountain
Stand and behold
the kingdom

Raise your sword
to the sun.
Turn to face
what you would not know

Sons of Adam
beat back the illusion,
give forth of life and,
stand at the chasm of being.

Sons of Adam
behold the daughters' of Eve
sitting in the valley of tomorrow
basking in the mid-day sun.

Give forth unto the daughters of Eve
for they hold the water of being
and the bread of life,
within they stand ready.

Daughters of Eve
raise your hands to the heavens,
see the stars.
Light is coming
Prepare yourselves.

Sons of Adam look
upon the countenance of Eve
for she prepares for new life.

Stand you daughters' of Eve
open your arms to the heavens
accept the experience of God.
Chaos will rein.

Daughters do not be in sorrow
you will bring forth new life,
new consciousness of being and
out of the chaos will come order.

Sons and daughters
face the sun,
soar to the stars,
sleep in purple moons.

Sons and daughters
go before
stand in love
rejoice for
the light of thy work returns.

December 29, 2007

Glory

Looking into the mystical mirror
The stars reflecting
I am all there is in this moment
I exist, I am, I am not

Rejoicing in the mystery
Singing in silence of Truth
Words untold of the coming
I am exists in this silence

Speaking in the silence
What is told, cannot
be heard by ears alone.
Be glad for Truth is coming.

Be jubilant for the stars
have predicted this coming
The fields sing and trees clap.
Shepherds know
the mystical silence filled with song

Proceed to the gate of Israel and
greet that which is to be
with great joy and peace.
No longer despair
For light returns unto you.

And your silence is filled with music.
Rejoice and sing
Let the silence ring with Peace
Know the existence of all I Am I

For in this we will know love
And in this we will know
the light of freedom.

Behold the babe is in the stars
The angels sing
The shepherds have known
Our entrance awaits.
Be thankful, rejoice for
The glory of I am cometh

Hear O yea
I am I exists as you.
let your silence be heard.
Be in grace
for today the babe cometh
in oneness, peace, joy, and love

The stars will be seen in your mirror
The angels will greet you singing of your existence
The Glory of I AM I will exist forever
never beginning and never ending.

For in this moment of silence
Truth is all there is.
Let me fall on my knees
And rejoice for today I am I
Nothing more and nothing less.

Let silence of the great unbound whole sing
for Peace returns in the light.

December 17, 2007

When God Whispers

I stand and turn
wrapped in the arms of the Absolute.
as I turn, I stand
in space above the earth
above the heavens
in the stars.

There is a great silence,
only silence,
only my own lifeforce
rushing in my ears
my being dilating
into the universe further and further.

Before the I Am I, I Am...
I am the silence,
the stars,
space and time,
the infinitude of God.

I pass through
the center of my soul
the fires gather
within my being rising
higher and higher,
further and deeper into space.

Taking me beyond all time,
beyond all silence,
beyond all infinitude.
burst through the top of God's head
life stands still.

In my arms is my child
for the first time
I see the face of God...
God Whispers I will be with thee
forever and ever
for today thee has brought forth in love.

for all my children
Spring 1998

Joy and sorrow are inseparable. . . together they come and when one sits alone with you . . . remember that the other is asleep upon your bed.

~Kahlil Gibran

Anguish

Mental pain, emotional let down seem to be connected to feelings of love. Perhaps these pains, these longings are how we recognize the joy and beauty of love. A relationship ends, and we find we are angry, hurt and have lost our way. Our hesitation at commitment is linked to the remembering of this anguish.

There are many things I can say to you about pain and consciousness and reflective consciousness, but in the end we don't heal until we acknowledge our hurt and pain and eventually let it go for new understanding of our life. In this process we learn to forgive, to give up the old for the new…

I Woke Up Angry At You

I woke up angry at you
Wanting to know why I should be alone
You have hurt me, I don't know where to turn.

How could you leave me and not tell me?
Where am I to find you?
I am angry at you this morning.

In my anger I have torn our pictures
Thrown our love items away
I am angry at you this morning.
How could you leave me like this?
What purpose is it being alone ?

There are hot tears falling on our table,
how I am ever to enjoy my food without you
I would smash all that reminds me of you
Tears are scalding my flesh
The flesh you loved and gave purpose to

Why did you take my very purpose of life
In your leaving you have left me numb
I am angry at you
I would rip my heart from my chest
Rather than allow it to long for you

There is no longer meaning in the moon on your pillow
I have slashed the pillow you slept on
I could not bear the moon showing me you had left

I will burn the swing where we made love
I am angry at you
You did not tell me what purpose
I am to have without you

I want to pluck my eyes from their sockets
Rather than have them look for you
I am angry at you
How will my eyes know meaning
Show me why I should be alone

The flowers that we grew in our love are gone
I have trampled them like you trampled my love for you
I am angry at you
Your promises all broken
Living without purpose in a dying garden
I will not wait to be in peace

I read the letters we wrote
I am angry at you
You lied to me it was not forever
I would burn your love into my mind forever
But you have taken it away from me
The forever you left me was pain

I am angry at you

November 10, 2007

Love Does Not Die

I do understand
you have ways of moving past this
Love does not die

You will never forget them
they have shaped the core of your being
Love does not die

All that was brought to your life
All that you shared will remain
Love does not die

Heart of stone now soften to the mere touch
You cant fool me
Love will not die

Your spirit wants to be known
As you enter into the being you are
You long to be loved
Love does not die

The anger must fade to tears
the hurt to healing
Love does not die

Actions have nothing to do with love
Meaning is steeped in the need to be known through love
Love does not die

You will not forget
You can't deny the beauty of your love
Love will not die
You will not die
for love does not die
Love brings the eternal flame of life
For Love does not die.

for Aaron
October 25, 2007

Waiting

13 Days until you arrive.
That is 308 hours… 18,480 minutes
and 1,180,800 seconds to wait.

This is an eternity,
my soul waiting to greet yours.
Slowly time seems to move toward an untold future.
Illusion clouds our reality
as our hearts are steeped in imagination.

Moments spent in quiet
now roar in my ears.
Silence no longer golden.
Waiting the whispers
of your being in my life.

18,475 minutes
and 1,108,500 seconds to wait.
An eternity of waiting agony

How will I know you?
Our hearts have met
Soul to soul we have talked
Whispers unheard this day
My life awaits your entrance.

18,465 minutes
and 1,107, 900 seconds to wait.
An eternity of waiting
agony

Food grows cold
Wanting to share with you
Seeing you at the table of my life
Sharing in the fruits we have grown
Awaiting the entrance of new being.

Torment of time and space
Whispering of illusions of time
Speaking of that which has never been
All that we have thought of no avail
What has been wished for will be known

10 days until you leave.
240 hours…
14, 400 minutes…
846,000 seconds
How will I survive the departure
And count the beginning we will build

December 10, 2007

An Ordinary Day

It feels like a rather ordinary day.
Nothing wonderful just the usual day
An ordinary day

Soft hazy fog floating through the trees
Saturday morning noises dampened
Nothing urges me on

Rolling to my side I reached for you
Your back moves from my touch
Shoulders shrugging you take a deep breath

Smells of last nights dinner float
And thoughts of unfinished chores arise
Nothing seems finished this morning

Dread rises into my throat and
Tears sting my eyes
I had almost forgotten what day this was

For three years we danced and laughed
Made love when we could
You told me I had changed you

Tears stream down my cheeks
My heart feels numb and dead
This is no ordinary day

My mind has a dozen reasons for you to stay
But it will do no good
You are going today

How civilized we are
Packing your belongings into the car
Do you have enough towels?

Tears race down my throat
Forcing a smile I hand you another pillow
Checking through the house for anything left

Boxes packed
Strained goodbyes said

I want to throw rocks at you
Instead I go back into our home
To live another ordinary day

November 17, 2007

Release Me

Pounding suffocating pain
Torment non-ending in this day
Stretched and pulled I will not survive the torture
Release me let me go

Pounding suffocating pain
How does one endure such hellish thoughts
Tormented once again by uncertainty
Release my flesh and let me go

Pounding suffocating pain
Eyes glazed from sights deaden in time
Tormented again by past deeds
Release me from this torture.

Pounding suffocating pain
How does one survive love
Tormented by words unsaid
Release me from this endless song

Pounding suffocating pain
Your very touch smolders in my mind
This love has left my flesh on fire
Release me and let me love you

Pounding suffocating pain
Torment unending in this day
Why won't you take my love
Release me so I may know peace

Pounding suffocating pain
Tortured by my desires to touch you
Wanting to know the depth of you
Release me so I may love you

Pounding suffocating pain
Tormented by my need to tell you
Tortured by the words you will not hear
Release me so I may speak ...

Endless pain of love not known
Tortured thoughts of uncertainty
Words drown in the torment of time
Pounding desire to be known

Release me

November 11, 2007

Road to Nowhere

We stood looking down the road
A road that leads to nowhere
living a life that can't be fixed
watching it pass us by

I want to fix you
but too much time has passed
I want a direction but
no signs are on this road to nowhere

Our future feels static
seems as if life passes us by
on this dusty road to nowhere
life is around and never touching us

I want to fix you
But seems like life is too long gone
how did we find ourselves here
On this road to nowhere

Finding direction
on this road to nowhere
did we ever know where we were going
do we know where we came from
does it matter if we don't know

I can't fix you… can't make it right
Can only let the static pass us by
We are on a road to somewhere

Broken and lost
we stand together
finding our road from nowhere
turning onto the road of somewhere

It cant be fixed
It is heavy on my mind
Its alright
To take a ride to nowhere

It has always been a road to nowhere

April 18, 2008

Lies

Lie and tell me you love me
You lied and told me you left the other behind
You lied and told me I was the only one
Lied when you kissed and held me

You lied when you made love to me
Telling me you were mine forever
Lied when we danced and you looked into my eyes
Lied and told me you had left your old life behind

Lies, lies, lies so you can lie one more time
Lie and tell me you love me

Lies about your undying love
Lies about our life together
You lied about your caring
Lied about your tears

Lies, lies, lies so you can lie one more time
Lie and tell me you love me

You lied and told me you loved my smile
Lies about me being in your dreams
You lied saying we would always find one another
Lies telling me we would sing all night

Lies, lies. lies so you can lie one more time
Lie and tell me you love me

You lied and told me you would never leave
Lies telling me that no one could take you from me
Lied saying your life would be over if I left
Lies, lies, lies, stop lying and tell me you love me.

December 3, 2007

Torture

Twisting in the moon,
blowing in the wind
torture because I wont be

Purified by the sun
cleansed by the water
tortured because I will not be

Kissed by the stars
touched by the dark velvet sky
tortured because I will not let it be

Sung in a song
danced in the meadow
tortured because I don't know how to be

Play me
sing me
dance with me
teach me to be
Love me
take me
teach me to be
hold me
touch me
teach me to be

Stand with me in a circle of fire so we may be

October 30, 2007

Just As Is

I am lost
I am nothing
here I stand
alone a woman

Just as is
body broken and tattered
wasted upon the winds of time
caught in my earthly reality
forced to survive in my secret cave
that I myself have dug

Just as is
A mind who knows not what
thoughts of life spent
caught in my own fantasy of life
forced to endure my thoughts
as a truth I created.

Just as is
heart that has known
love unending
love spent on never ending
wanting
craving
caused by my momentary insanities
a soul, a woman in search of peace.

March 24, 2008

Yesterday's Sacrifice

Purple opaque scars
Feelings and pangs of regret
don't tell the story
only the pain I have known

Regression and sorrow
progression without thought
life without pause
purple opaque scars

Pause
Think
Exist for this moment
quaint qualms

A slave to my scars
purple opaque lines
attaching me to the pain
just stop a minute

Exist for this moment only
pause, think, exist
slave to my addiction
of pain and hurt

Haunted by my past
tasting the time that wears
behind my flesh
no sacred place to flee

Dead space
wasted tissue
rattling bones within a shell
purple opaque scars

Pause a moment
think for this time
silent confusion
progression backward

can you feel me?

March 23, 2008

Wasting Away

Here I am wasting away
thought it would be alright
wasted love on
winding streets of the metropolis

Wasting away
connections lost
secluded goals
shattered in the dank gray

Same hopes as yesterday
endowed at dawn
gray streaks wasting the sun
still no purpose

Endless concrete
long walk home
wasting away on the
city's gray paths

Wasting away
taunted by windows closed
tainting my soul for a season
endless concrete

Suspended personalities
strolling aimless
life not sensed
senses not seen

Endless concrete
no purpose
something last night
wasting away

April 23 2008

Dark City Night

Stepping into the darken city
mist flows around me
run to the phone
but it does not ring
I cannot find you

Stepping into the eternal mist
dissolving myself into being
run for the mail
it does not come
I cannot find you

Stepping into the darkened room
empty chairs that would not be
empty thoughts I cannot have
I cannot find you

Bring me from this darken city
bring me from this darken room
please find me

Reach me
touch me
dance with me
bring me into being

December 3, 2007

Where Has My Passion Gone

Where has my passion gone this day?
I awoke in a grey haze feeling numb
wanting to reach out to you
and feel our passion
but you were not there

How am I know our passion this day
the grey surrounds the trees and the houses
my fingers do not find you
the fire of passion is dampened
the very source of fire is lost in the grey

Numbness spreads through my limps
fingers not knowing
not reaching the fire
cold steel existing where
fires once burned freely.

Where has my passion gone this day?
How could I loose you among the
trees and houses
grey spreading over all there is…
Grey haze everywhere

Go
Let my fires return
for my love awaits me.

November 19, 2007

Please Don't Love Me

I had looked for you forever
Watching your wonderful face
while you sleep.
Enchanted by
the softness of your being,
feeling your skin in a kiss.

No one warned me
or told me about this in you.
It should be easy
to let you go.

We could have our fling,
laugh a little, and
have some great sex.

How was I to know there would be love.
You shouldn't have let me love you so.
Don't love me this hurts too much.

Rolling over looking at the wall
tears welling in my eyes.
In 10 days you will leave
going home again,
the fling done. Agony.

My body throbs to know you more
each time we touch.
There is this place we are headed for,
once we reach it we cannot easily escape
the destiny we have chosen.

Please, please dont love me
there is too much pain in this love we are building.

Feeling you stir beside me
you reach around and pull me too you.
Small kisses on my neck
soft light strokes
produce shudders of pleasure

Turning to look into your eyes
and melt into your lips.
Heart upon heart,
flesh upon flesh
swiftly moving to a chasm of no return.
My being parts so easily for you now.

Please don't abandon me to this love we are living.

Dear God give me one more day
in this place I have found.
Help me to be here forever.

No one told me such pleasure would come
with this depth of torment.
The candle flickers in response,
quiet shadows play across your face
as you slumber beside me.

Vigil will be kept tonight.
You have taken me to a place
only imagined in my fantasy.

This place we rest in has become sacred.
How will I endure your leaving?

Double Chocolate   Suzanne Deakins
Will the echoes destroy my sanity?
Please don't make me love you so
the agony is too much.

The muted sound of the shower reaches my ears.
Having fallen asleep the vigil lost.
Is it you in the shower?
Are you preparing to leave already?
No not today we have 9 more days.

Pulling the covers to my head
for today we will remain in our sacred spot.

Your quiet steps upon the floor,
covers gently pulled back,
being pulled to your warm body.
Snuggling we fold into each other
as our passion mounts our consciousness.

Let this one memory
be burned into my mind forever.
Let this never end mantra and prayer.
As we reach the stars
there are tears again.

Tears mixed with pain,
tears mixed in pleasure.
Don't let me love you so much.

Where did the days go?
Tomorrow you leave.
Someone should have warned me about you.

How was I to know
I would love you so much.
No one warned me of the

agony of this kind of love.
No one warned me
you would never let me be.
You have created this hunger in me.
This hunger only you can satisfy.

Someone should have warned me about you.
Please, please don't make me love you so much.

The coffee cannot wake me
as we prepare to leave for the airport.
How will I be able to drive home
without you beside me?

You made sure last night
I would never forget you.
Your naked body burned into
my mind forever,
your marks upon my flesh making me yours.

Who will want me now?
I have been given to you in totality.
Every pore,
very atom of my being
has your name etched into it.

My mind is weak in wanting you.
Why must I love you so.
One last wave and scalding tears falling…
please don't love me so much.

Just one more day and
one more kiss.

November 26, 2007

Wandering

Wandering around in this vast,
dark
endless space,
and I wonder.
about life,
death,
all and none.
Thinking of love,
hate,
everything so nothing.

Experiencing the shadows,
the flame,
I wonder about the fire,
water,
air, and earth...
I am a wonderer.
destined for the paradox throughout life.

Without a hope,
a goal,
this is my destination.
Everywhere,
nowhere.
This is my sorrow.

Is there a light,
in this dismal void.
Questioning truth in this ignorant place.
Can there be love without feeling?

This is the of life.
The reason neither For nothing.
Yearning yearn to feel nothingness..
tortured no light,
no hope,
no feeling,
just shadows,
just a wandering

This is the sorrow
of life.
The reason there is no longing.
neither for life or death.
For nothing.

Yearning for peace.
yearn to be nothing,
feeling nothingness..
tortured existence…
no light,
no hope,
no feeling,
just shadows,
just a wandering soul… amidst nothing.

November 11, 2000

All I really need is love, but a little chocolate now and then doesn't hurt!

~Author Unkown

Soft Kisses

Soft kisses, soft love leaves a warm glow like a cup of hot chocolate on a cold night in front of a fireplace. Not all affairs are passionate ending in agony. It has been my experience that long time love affairs have many moments of softness of sharing simple things like gardens, books, and a cup of tea or coffee.

Often when a liaison starts softly it grows passionate later. Sometime when a fire is too hot it consumes everything around it and quickly burns itself out. Love can be this way too much fire or passion and it burns itself out... leaving the lovers cold and in pain... But soft kisses are a salve.

Have I Told You I Love You?

Have I told you I love you?
Today when I woke
I knew you would be there
I reached and held you close

My fingers gently stroking you
Touching you with love
How can I tell you what I am feeling?

The words that come
Do not reveal the depth
How can words reveal the heart?

Heart can be known only to heart.
My fingers gently stroking your love
Reaching for that which has not been known

I knew you would come into my life
Our love is spreading through the very being
There is no lines of beginning and ending.
Melding into the love of each other

We have found what we did not know
Passing from one to another
Forever attached at the heart

Reaching through the illusion of self
Have I told you I love you?
Going beyond the pain of separation.

Finding the secret of existence
Touching the love you are.
I love you

January 28, 2008

When We Touch

Sometimes when we touch,
Sometimes I think of you
Sometimes you think of me
And when this happens at the same time
we connect and don't know it.

You protected yourself
and could not love me
I protected myself and
could not surrender to you.

Unspoken plans
Unknown desires
Closeness
Softness
Holding hands

Making love at strange times
Afraid to let go of the passion
Holding it all very close
Plans without hurry
looming in our future.

I don't know what love is
And you don't answer me

Snuggling close
Wanting to understand the desire
And lack of desire
Wanting you to come
Wanting you to wait

I don't know what love is
And you don't answer me
Desire unending
Desire not beginning.

Holding hands
Across space
When I think of you
And you of me
We connect.

January 3, 2008

Softly Last Night

I felt you softly last night
Embracing my being
lightly caressing my mind
pulling me to you.

Stepping lightly this morning
wanting to understand our
growing love
softly going forward into my day

Surprised at the depth of
new feelings
embracing the beginnings
seeing you in the morning light

Softly going into my life
wanting you to be there
needing you beside me
knowing this is a new existence

Loving you this morning
allowing the depth of love to be known
experiencing love lightly in my life

Softly stepping into our future
knowing each thought
brings us closer to the experience of love
Gently tirring the love we are

Softly coming into my love of you

February 1, 2008

The Joining

Slowing turning, turning
softly dilating, turning, slowly turning to meet the sun.
Slowly turning to meet the cool water
turning slowly to meet you... to meet your eyes
turning again to meet your soul.

Turning, slowly turning with the sun on my skin
and the moon in my eyes.
Turning in the softness of love to see the stars...
turning to see the sun on the trees
and the breeze in the leaves.

Miraculously I have not lost you.
Turning that I might give my being to yours.
Turning in the softness of love...
I have found myself in this moment.

Turning, slowly turning...
feet moving upon the velvet of the earth.
Feet on the velvet path to your heart.
Turning, slowly turning...
to meet the joy of your heart and soul.

Hearing your voice upon breeze bringing me love.
I have not lost you in this moment of turning.
I have found our love.

Softly turning... dilating to meet your touch,
a touch of all time and space...
velvet touch of the earth.
turning, softly turning to be touched and loved.
Velvet path to my heart and soul wanting to be touched.

Slowly turning to touch you...
softly turning, to ride the breeze
and bring you words of my love.

Slowly turning, miraculously you have not lost
me in this moment of turning.
Slowly turning as I see you find yourself
in this moment of my love.

Slowly turning so that you may meet my eyes
and find my soul.
Softly turning so that the sun will be on your skin
and the moon in your eyes.

Softly turning so that we shall be as one.
Blending, turning, and being as one being...
accepting and giving,
moving in the passion of the stars.
Slowly turning the passion of love
soft breezes bring the music of love
turning, softly turning...
moving toward infinity...
turning, softly turning on the edge of all time...
being one without ending.

Passion in your eyes fills my soul...
softly turning... passion in my eyes reaches for your
soul...
one being is born.
One love softly turning to know itself as one...
One love for all eternity... slowly turning to know all love

Softly turning for all time,
turning, throbbing to the rhythm of all time
accepting and giving being as one love and life

throbbing passion filling our lives.
Hearts in unison throbbing to the tides of life…
bodies wanting of eternity the longing of touch
touching for an infinity throbbing in passion
throbbing to know all that is to be.

Throbbing in passion of being
in this passion we have known as one being…
and brought forth in love
we have multiplied our love in this obsession of love.

We have created the heavens and the earth…
and the unending of music of life
Slowly turning, turning to know all that is in our love…
softly touching and breathing …
slowly turning to meet your eyes.
Turning, slowly turning so that you may meet my eyes.

Softly dilating to meet
what we have brought forth in love…
softly turning to meet the creation of love as one being.
We shall be forever for we have brought forth in love.

January 2000

Separated and Cloven

Separated by time
Separated by space
into two we stand
upon the path to nowhere.

Separated by time
Separated by space
into two we stand
upon the path to somewhere

Separated by time
Separated by space
into two we have become
searching for someone.

Separated by thought
Separated by desire
into two we have become.

searching for the one that we could become
Separated by illusion
Separated by dreams
dreaming of the one not two.

Searching in the twilight for the sun
Searching for the star you are
Searching for the moon upon our bed
Cloven and alone... no more

October 16, 2007

On My Mind

You were on my mind
awakening from sweet dreams
snuggled in soft covers
smelling your being

You were on my mind
eating breakfast
reading the paper
drinking my coffee

Your energy sat
across the table
smiling and just being
softly accepting our life.

Distance
Space
Time
Keeps us from touching

Your absence keeps me
in an unknown reality
loving your energy
craving your being

Desiring a life with you
small things
food
gardens
walks

Yearning for your touch
longing for kisses soft
passionate wanting
flesh against flesh

I hear your voice
and I can not speak
my heart raises to my throat
cheeks flushed
heart pounding

How can there be space?
time stands still
all that has been
dreaming of your smile

feeling your energy
simple moments
flights of fantasy
lost in these moments of you

You are always on my mind

March 11, 2008

Secrets

Be still so you may hear
Be quiet my love
I have a secret to tell you

Quiet your pounding heart so you may hear me
Close the curtains so no one may see
I have a secret to tell you

Let go of your busy work my love
Let your hands and mind rest
I have a secret to tell you

Let us go into the garden
Sit upon the bench and watch the leaves fall
I have a secret to tell you

See the blue jay fly high
Do you see the squirrel hiding its nuts
Quietly my love
I have a secret to tell you

Quietly my love let my wings enfold you
Let our stars guide my love
For our secret is so dear
I have a secret to share with you
Soar with me
Be with me

I have a secret to tell you
My secret is simply my love
Listen quietly so you will know
My secret is I love you…

October 5, 2007

4th Day of Christmas

Friends gathering
eating and sharing food
warmth of existence
Long walks in the rain
River waters running strong
Clouds running wild

Cold nights bundled up
slipping out of clothes
under down covers
Icy fingers touching
flesh seeking to be warm
Enfolding into each other

Listening to the rain
pounding on the roof as
small snores fill the silence
Scent of life fills the air
Sea foam dreams float by
as sand castles drift among the waves

Discovering you under
blue filtered lights
going to edge of all
endless deep kisses
being wrapped in your consciousness
scents of tomorrow linger on
Spark of existence
Spark of life
Beginning known
Flesh giving life
flesh accepting creation
realization embraced   *December 27, 2007*

113

Winter's Coming

Winds of winter whispering
Snow gently falling
Frost covered windows
A warm bed with you

Rolling over to feel your back
Arms flung over you pulling
your flesh to mine
heat of desire warming us.
Soft desire beckons

Opening us to this morning
Soaking in rosemary oil
Watching the clouds run.
Each day brings me
Closer to the edge of you

Pushing back
Once more seeing
Quiet thoughts
of lusty moments
steeped in magic
and dreams
Deep velvet kisses
Electric moments of touch

Deep sighs
Flashing lights
Finding the rhythm
Your body next to mine
touching in the glow of dawn

Purple moons fluttering
Throbbing melodious song
Heart on wing
Snowbirds falling

Floating in the sea of sexuality
Gentle roaring of the waves
Soft entrance into my being
Consummated in love.

December 25, 2007

The Coming Fog

I went looking for you
upon the path to your rabbit hole,
but the fog blocked my way.
Swirling and touching
the sky it laid heavily
upon the stones...

I could not find our table
or my teapot or our cups...
the fog lay upon them all.
upon the path to your rabbit hole,
but the fog blocked my way.

The fog is laying upon the trees
and covering the flowers
Have you taken our cups
and tea pot into your rabbit hole?
Have you lit the candles and laterns
so we may see again?

I went looking for you
upon the path to your rabbit hole,
but the fog blocked the moon
and the stars.
It swirled around me
I could not see you.
The fog swirled upon my face,
leaving cold droplets of mist in my eyes.
Our path seems to float
in this misty light upon my eyes.
Will you dry the mist so I may find you?

for WR   *October 28, 2007*

Eclipse

I saw you tonight
slowly slipping into the dark
sliding beyond my sight
hiding behind what I could not see

I saw you tonight
peeking at me from afar
silver light
hard to see when I first looked for you
High above the lights of the city
Through rain covered windows
What will be as you are revealed?

Stars are dimmed by your light
the grass is filled with diamonds
and the sun bows before you.
I saw you tonight peeking at me
Silver light filling my garden
laying your purple traps
Leaving your chocolate for me to taste
I saw you tonight waiting in the bamboo and roses…
making shadows to tease me.

You slip so easily behind
the wispy clouds
throwing your light
leaving me yearning
How easily you are
amused upon my pillow
and playing across the windows
setting my room aglow with
secrets.

I saw you peeking at me   *for Acara February 20, 2008*

Last Year

Last year I knew
your phone number
the sound of your voice sent
chills of anticipation through my flesh

Last year there were no tears
I would have sold my soul
to be with you
I knew your blood and heart

Last year I felt you breathe
in and accept my love
Breathe out and give love

You said touch me
feel me
my heart beats and I bleed
Last year I knew you

I went to call you
the number has left
my mind
the feeling left my flesh

Can't seem to get inside your head
to know what to do
you are in my head
don't want to let you go
s
Last year I felt your flesh
next to mine

your scent filled my
being with promise
can't stop sensing you
Last year I yearned
to be held and known
running through the
garden we grew

Can't get you out of my
being… our love
lingers and covers me
growing like our new life

Last year we walked
in the rain
watched the clouds
and spoke of us

Your words fill me
caress me at unknown
moments in life
giving me hope

Last year I knew you
breathing in life
your heart beat
and your soul glowed
Last year I knew you.

for Andy
July 17, 2008

To Really Love A Woman

To really love a woman
You have to understand her
Look into her eyes
See her soul

To really love a woman
You have to let her go
Let her come
Look into her soul

To really love a woman
You have to let her cry
Hold her gently in your arms
Stroke her into sleep
Give her the right to love
And to laugh

Give her the entrance to your heart
Cast off that role that keeps you away
To really love a woman
You have to accept lonely
and give your heart
let her know you will never leave

Let her know she is the
the only one you want
To really love a woman
let her in to your heart

To really love a woman
make it all right
fly with her in the wildest dreams
be her hero

To really love a woman
you have to have
the soul of a woman
you have to moon dance

To really love a woman
Take her in your arms
Promise her to love her forever
Give her your word the pain is gone.

To really love a woman
Love her more than life
to stay there until life is through
Unable to leave...

To really love a woman
Surrender to your love
Surrender your heart,
your body, and soul

Near and far
Never let her go

May 1, 2008

What Did You Expect of Me

You came into my life,
unannounced
unaware of the tides and stars in my life.
Your energy took me by surprise
strong ...innocent
filled with pain.

Is it possible to be in pain
and yet innocent?
How was I not to love your eyes
and smile
Yes I want you,
I want you to want me.

Where have you taken my heart
touching my soul.
Can you be held with the wings?
Can you be tethered to earth
you soar above me
teasing me with your spirit

You have turned my sky blue
put rainbows in my eyes
Will I keep you in my life...
and what happens if you fly away to another.

Will you leave me with a feather from your wings?
Will you teach me to soar before you go?
How will I love from afar...

how am I not to love you?
What do you expect of me?

Of course I want you.
Come into my dream
or in my day time,
I care not, just come to me.

Rest with me for a moment
so I may see the stars in your eyes
and hear the tales of far off places.
How do you want me to love you?

And if I love you what will you do?
You with the wings
you have stolen my heart.
Where did you take it?
Yes I want you to want me.
I want you to love me,
take me and teach me to fly with you.

If I fly with you what is to become of my life?
Will I still go to work each day?
Still live in this life I have created?
What do you want me to do soaring one..

How does one sleep upon the earth
once you have flown in the stars?
Did you think I would not know who you are?
What did you expect of me.

If I want you with all of my heart
and soul will you stay with me?
Will we be allowed to love
and if we love what will happen?

You with the wings,
please give me back my heart.
What did you expect of me,
wanting you
wanting you to want me.

You have taught me to fly
if only for a second.
What is to become of me
without you...

You with the wings take me to the moon.
Give me wings that I may always fly with you...
What do you expect ...
how am I not to love you?

Come take me with you to the stars,
let me hear the angels sing in your whisper... of course I
want you.

November 15, 2008

Timeless Love

Timeless love you fill me up
Playing me along the waves
Sweeping me among the clouds
Laying the path to my heart
You fill me up

Drawing me to your stream of love
Unknown sounds fill my ears
Unseen sights fill my eyes
Timeless love you fill me up

January 19, 2008

Hush Sweet Love

Hush my lover
Come to me
Silently into my heart
Calmly into my arms

Gently my lover
My sweet love
Shed the skin
You hide beneath

How bad could it be
To fall in love with me
To amuse yourself with me
Sexuality how bad could be

Release me
Free me from this chastity
Set my life aside
Gently my lover love me

My dreams went flying by
My eyes stayed on your soul
Taking a chance on us
How bad could it be to love me

Hush my sweet love
Come gently to my arms
Let me take a chance
On loving you.

See me shed my tears
My life goes flying
Wanting to know you

Hush sweet lover
Taking a chance on loving you
How bad could it be
Breaking the chains of chastity
Sexuality how bad could it be

Hush my lover
Come gently into my arms
Take a chance on love

How bad could it be...

April 2008

You Gently Filled My Life

You came gently into my life
filling my senses with softness
allowing me time to be
embracing my being with tenderness

You stirred my fires of being
heating up the very idea
that I might find love
as you filled me gently with love

You filled me with your laughter
bringing me to the point of
acceptance of the idiocy
I would have thrown out

You filled me with hope
filling me to the brim
with courage knowing I could continue
You filled my senses gently
with the scent of spring
and the colors of new life
the wanting

You filled me with strength
taking me to brink of
a crevice of sanity
You filled me up
every atom every cell
you taught me to soar
to be as never before

Filling up my senses
with the very being
fusing my heart to yours

You filled me up
with the inevitable
desire of humanity seeking to know

You filled me up
with the touch
of your flesh on my flesh
You filled me with your words
giving me the timeless
craving
of understanding

Your humanity filled my senses
smelling your flesh
feeling the silk of your being
looking into your eyes
You filled my human life
keeping me from wandering
seeking no more
for flesh has found flesh

As you fill me up
life has found life
soul has found soul
and being is fulfilled.

February 25, 2008

You Touched Me

You touched me
I felt you touch me
I know you did not want me to know
but I felt it
you touched me

I remember the first time
hearing your name
feeling your touch
seeing you smile
and you touched me

You looked at me
and my heart was in my throat
my flesh on fire
have I lost my mind?
surrendering to you in this way

Slowing undressing each other
Waiting for my breath
How am I to breathe without
your touch?

I have no existence without your touch
Laying in each others arms
softly talking desiring
and not knowing
turning on my side so I can see your beauty
knowing it may not last

You touched me
I felt you touch me
I know you did not want me to know
but I felt it you touched me

There are moments
my desire rages within me
wanting out
wanting to be loved by you
my knees go weak when
I think of you touching me

Will you dare to understand
Are you capable of letting it be
Do you have the strength
to let my fingers find
your soul and heart?

It feels as if I have waited
forever for these moments
do not be afraid for you have touched me
I know you did not want me to know
But I felt it you touched me.

Take my hand
walked with me in the rain
feel the warmth
lay naked with me in the sun
speak to me of the stars
dance with me in the water
softly come to our being

For you have touched my heart and soul

February 16, 2008

Money talks, chocolate sings
~Author Unknown

The Dawn of Consciousness

Each of us holds a piece of life that holds all the purpose, meaning and infinity of being. This consciousness is constantly growing and unfolding, bringing meaning and purpose to the one moment we have. Like the softness of dawn this consciousness plays upon our being. We have only to stop, get quiet and let it reveal its beauty to us.

The only thing you need to do is become present in the-NOW... quiet the ego mind... and allow the dawn to unfold in your life. It is my experience that we can love everyone we are aware of... intentional love, intentional consciousness. To love is the same choice as to hate... it is a conscious decision we make.

Perceived In Ink

Perceived only in the ink
The blank page tells our story
No imagination, no being

Ink stained hands reaching to touch the existence of life
The blank page tells our story
How am I to make my marks
Will my ink stained fingers leave their print

Is our existence only in the ink
Will we be known only on this page
No words, no being
Ink stained fingers reaching to know

Reveal your being
Allow my page to be full
Leave your ink print upon my life
Fingers that are writing the story

Come to me maker of stories
Reveal your secret life to my book
Leave none of my pages empty
Creator of my story leave your ink upon me

I would know this ink,
No matter what it writes
I crave its words and being
Come to me ink stain
Give me meaning

November 15, 2007

What Between

What blue stars?
What mad raving?
What sights, what sounds!
What lovely realities abound for the unchained mind!

Being without end
Life without beginning
Thought without thought
Free at last

No longer chained
Free of earthbound sight
Heavenly sounds filling the spaces between
Free at last

Shadows to light
Rainbow to white
Heavenly quiet filling the spaces between
Free at last

Heart to Heart
Fear to embracement
Unbound whole
Free at last

Love without ending
Peace where torment once reined
Filling the spaces between
Free at last to be.

for Spiral Jetty   *December 7, 2007*

I Am Human

I am a human
all of those things never mentioned,
I am human
an unopened package with a heartbeat
containing, body, mind, and soul
I am a human
I have transparent flesh
built with an opaque wrapper

I am a human
translucent feelings carrying
hidden truths within
I am a human that holds many personalities
each bearing the masks of the truth I know to be

I am a human
committing actions that hold within untold secrets
unsung echoes; returned from an unnamed cave in space,
found only in the furthest vertical, horizontal, timelessness
conquering the world, conquering self, becoming that
becoming what is, becoming each object that is to be
becoming.

I am a human
all life, is whispered to me in the middle of the night
I am thoughts erupting from the soul of the earth
I am that which follows that which was first
I am human
I am flesh
I am rocks formed by the hand of the divine
I am the sand
I am spirit
I am free
I am love
I am human

March 9, 2008

This Is Not A Love Story

This is not a love story
But a tale of those who
give in to love
living a vision

We have confused a fairytale
With the craving of the soul
and longing of the heart
to be branded by another

We put on our masks
and take false names.
Adorning our consciousness
with roles suited to the
fantasy of the love myth
we danced.

A rather mundane life
made into an astonishing
story of love existing in
a shocking reality

We believed it was a love story
a story we wanted
dreams dancing
under the masks of the ball.

The music stops
and lights go out
and our masks are
dropped one last time

This is the love story
we wrote in our dreams
danced in our fantasy
and finally accepted as our own.

April 23, 2008

Ode to Zero

You stood there as if you had value
Making me feel as if I needed you
you have no meaning
without the one

Singing your praises
walking to your point
knowing that all that is
is what exists

Wondering at your illusion
seeking to know your totality
never changing
needing only one

Existence without beginning
or ending
has nothing ever not existed?
Can that which has no existence be?

Is all that is, that which is?
The appearance does not
change the perception and
perception based on nothing
can have no existence.

Perception based on one
is…
the appearance does not change
the perception, for
that which is, has always been.

Step out of your place
let me into that spot
where none other
has ever existed.
Stop standing there without meaning.

March 27, 2008

When Did The Dream Leave

I don't know when
I realized the dream was over
the longing in my heart
tears in my eyes

The dream has come and gone
I keep waiting for you
waiting for the birds to sing
biding time in the clouds

Hearing the crows call
Been waiting for you in the bamboo
wind blowing in the trees
weeds dried and cracked

I don't know when the dream
went away on the clouds
Stumbling in the dark
Waiting for you in the corner

What am I to do with my heart
I don't know when the dream stopped
how do I let you go
Where do I put the dream in my mind

When the birds come and say your name
What do I tell them,
How will the clouds know how to be
When did the dream end
Light has gone
Stumbling in the dark
Waiting for the dream to come back

May 15, 2008

Standing In Love

Softly reaching out
through the haze of space
touching you.
Reaching through the wall
to know you are there.
Parting the haze of disbelief
touching you.

Heart beating as my fingers
reach you in anticipation.
Unbelievable that you exist

Softly reaching
through the haze of space
touching you.
Reaching through all time
to know you are there.

Clouds of disbelief roll past,
soul knowing you as
my fingers touch you face.
Standing in this place
Holding onto your being
Loving you in the mist of love.

for Randy
August 31, 2000

Everywhere At Once

Everywhere at once
Raging and still while I fear and want
Am I being the dream I have dreamt?
Will I find myself in the middle of this place of all times

Everywhere at once it is still and yet rages within me
Standing on the brink of chaos
Leaning into the chasm of insanity
How long must I stand as stone locked into not being

Everywhere at once flowing, oscillating, not being
Standing in the middle of nowhere
Existing in the middle of not being
What have I created in my dream

Everywhere at once eons of being and not knowing
Standing in the middle of my dream
Dancing in the middle of our dream
Raging stillness covers my very being

Everywhere at once stillness and raging
Flowing and being as I move to the middle of all life
Opening and being slowly I turn and look
Is this the final dream?

Slowly turning and facing the light of time
Where has this dream gone
Flowing into the center of the light
Retreating to the rage within

Standing on the brink of all life
Slowly turning and unfolding my wings
For I will soar into the rage and stillness
The stone has gone and only the dream remains

November 5, 2007

Have I Told You

Does this day bring joy to your heart?

Have I told you who I am?
Have I asked you who you are?
Does this day bring joy to your heart?

Did you know that the stars were perfect at your birth?
Did you know that I could sit in your mind forever?
Did you know there is place in my soul for you?

Is there a sacred place you go?
Will you go with me to mine?
Will you take me to God?
Will you let me take you to God?

Did you know that ever beat of music
brings me to your essence?
Did you know you have captured my being
with your essence?

Did you know we can fly?
Have your questions been answered?
Will you let me love you as consciousness?

Will you let me give you my words?
Have I told you this day brings joy to my heart?

November 19, 2007

Unconditional Love

We assume love is an answer
to our longings
wanting to feel desired and accepted.
Seeking validation
Warmth and acceptance of gestation

Desiring of acceptance of being
Striving for greater experience of being
Pain of birth
Afraid of rejection
Reaching out to touch life

Orgasmic moments of creation
To know God without prejudice
Pure sensual energy of creation
Prolonging moments of love

The flow of God
Unconditional love
All there is
Being knowing all
As love, as sensual life

November 27, 2007

This Morning

This morning I woke
snuggling down for a moment
letting the life of the day
into my consciousness

Throwing back the covers
silken air caressed my skin
light filled my mind
and scents of summer entered my lungs

Soft music filled me
touching every molecule
sending every atom vibrating
life itself moving and
swirling within my consciousness

The very moment of life
bringing joy and smiles
expressing as love
embracing all that has been,
will be and is

How blessed is this moment
this surrender to the
cosmic intent of life
to be known only
as consciousness

To be known
to be touched by love
even in small short moments
to make love as consciousness
with all those we meet

Life filling us
bringing us to the edge
of eternity
all that would be known
changes…

joy is the air,
laughing with the music
embracing this beingness
Joy unto the world this morning

Filled with love and caring
Embraced by God
And directed by cosmic intent.
Joy to us this day.

July 31, 2008

On Being Human

My flesh aches to know all there is today
Mind wondering through the forest
looking for signs of life
flesh seeking flesh
life seeking life

Wondering through my life
Seeking touch to know
How is one to know without touch
Seeking touch to be

Looking through my life
Seeking to know my being
Accepting my being as one
mind expressing as body

Mind seeking body
Mind in the hunt for Mind
Searching life as mind
Knowing life as body
Knowing to be

Urge to create new life abounds
Body in the quest for body
Flesh desiring flesh
Heart longing to be known
Yearning to be

Seeking immortality
Flesh wanting to touch
Tongue seeking to taste
That which will always be
Tasting to be

Body craving sight
Reaching beyond to see all that is
Yearning to be one with what is seen
in search of being
Seeing to be

To know God
To be human
Oneness as human seeking
Being as human knowing
This time for being fully human
Human knowing to be

December 15, 2007

Explantion of Work

The Priestess and Desire are works that came out of in-
tense moments where I was working on my conscious
awareness of happenings in my life. In the end all of this
work is about love and compassion, a rather extraordinary
kind of love. What good is understanding, knowing, wis-
dom, and awareness if we lack love and compassion?

To be a truly consciously aware being means to feel com-
passion and love for all that appears in your life, for in
reality this is your consciousness and if you cannot love
it... you cannot heal... or be in peace. Even that which
seems reasonable to hate and despise is only rescued from
the wells of insanity by wisdom surrounded with love and
compassion. Wrongs are not righted by wars, we are not
made safer through violence... we are, however, rescued
from these worldly concerns through love, compassion,
and wisdom.

To understand the nature of consciousness is to fully em-
brace life as a creation of your own creator self... to love
all that appears in the most sacred way.

July 24, 2008
West Linn, Oregon

The Priestess

Truth is that which is so,
that which is not Truth is not so,
therefore Truth is all there is.

The depth of the lake
beyond imagination this morning
bridges across are all filled with mist.
I have no sight to bring me across
the waters of life. Stepping slowly
upon the bridge,
money for the troll in hand,
herbs for the magic in my pocket,
in trepidation in my soul,
wondering and wondering
will I be strong enough to withstand this journey?

The bridge is gone
lost within the waters,
no money for the troll
no herbs for the magic.
Time and again
I feel I will drown
waters swallow me
washing over
pushing me down deeper and deeper.

My vision is clouded
sight is lost as deeper
into the darkness descending,

all breath gone,
vision lost for an eternity,
my soul screaming
in my mind.
Screaming for life and light,
love and compassion.
It finds none in this moment of darkness.

Within the scream is a sob
for all that could have been.
This sob turns to a great wrenching and gnashing
a pulling within my soul.
Blessed quietness… death
I am no more,
finally the act has been committed.

The crone has answered my scream
She brings me to the doorstep of death.
There is no fire here,
no water,
no air,
no earth
only eternal death.
She tells me to step across the threshold,
and I falter
trip and cry
for I am so afraid
of a deeper darkness,
which will come.
Stepping I am no more.

In this eternal death
there is no pressure to live.
I like this death this non me,

this no more to be.
Perhaps choose to stay here and not leave.
In this the darkness is soft, quiet and sensual.
Yes there is feeling here,
no blankness no hurt,
feeling starting to surge here.
A small heartbeat has occurred now
and in this life is slowly returning.

The high Priestess has called me and said,
"this is enough" she awaits me.

I cry for in this death
is my first peace.
Not wanting to leave here,
but stay eternally dead, quiet without life.
Fearing the awaiting life.
My vision has been one of drowning,
made misty by the intensity of the pain of life.
I do not want to know Truth or God,
only to remain dead without life now,
no more, just dead.

It is too late; the
Priestess has found me
with her eternal candle.

There is now a quickening within my soul.
I ask the Priestess to hold me
and she says "no."

She tells me I am not fully formed
and must not be touched yet
but by myself.
I cry for in this is a freedom.

Slowly growing in this dark place
the Priestess has prepared for me.
She has brought before me
many things I must see.
Weeping once again
Finding myself afraid of the water
of trolls and lack of magic.
Wishing not to have this sight.

Turning to run from it
The Priestess is everywhere.
There is no escaping my soul.
It is speaking again and
will not let me be dead.
It has joined with the Priestess
to preserve this in me,
this sight I would run from.

I have not yet spoken,
the Priestess encourages my voice.
Taunting me with sight to speak of it.
She makes my soul yearning to be heard.

Finally I begin to speak of Truth
that would not die in me,
of the eternal death and birth
I saw and am.

Weeping for I do not want
to see these things or speak of them.

The troll will hear
and take away the bridge
or charge me a fee I cannot pay.

My herbs are gone
My magic is no more.

Weeping for the fear of it all.
The Priestess tells me
tears are not voice
crying more for I have never used this voice.
She asks of me ...voice and
I am afraid it will boom
awakening the trolls and
I have no magic.
Crying for the fear of it all.

Slowly hearing
the voice come forth.
It is quiet and gentle in its sound,
behind it is raises a great fire.
More fire than I could have imagined.
My soul is now crying wanting me to reach
and touch the fire
holding back afraid it will scream
awaken the trolls.

Once again the Priestess must tell me
that tears are not voice.
She will not touch me for I am not fully formed.

Again wanting to return to death
to an eternity of darkness and solitude.
My soul will not allow this

My soul has come in my side door.
It has given me Sight.
All along it has been growing

loosing the mistiness of the water
keeping itself hidden so I would not destroy it.
Quickening unknown to me.

Weeping afraid of what it will make me see
the Priestess tells me once more this is not voice.
Asking for my magic back before I look
she says no. The magic is no more.
I cry and she laughs at the tears
and cries at the joy she says I will know.

Asking the Priestess to take me to a place most high
she says no. You are not fully formed.
You have lived by the earth, trolls and magic.
You have made your self dead by the waters
now you must know the fire
before there is the breath of life.

I cry and fear the pain of the fire.
The Priestess laughs and says, that was not fire you knew.
It was not your fervor it was the nether land of magic.

Not believing her and begging
allowed to turn to death
soul screams and runs to the Priestess for protection.
I cry and she tells me this is not voice.

As I turn to the Priestess
becoming fully consumed by the fire.
Screaming in fear and she says this is not voice.
Weeping and she says this is not voice.

Water in my sight is gone
only light is left.
Sight has spoken and she says this is voice.
Laughing for the joy of it all.

Asking her to touch me
she says no, you are not fully formed.
I cry and she reminds me voice is sight.
Stopping I say give me my magic
she says no more you will live
by life not by the earth or the water or the fire.
You have breath

Trying to cry
Finding there are no tears,
for my voice has changed.

The Priestess smiles
sends me back my soul
tells me I am not fully formed.
Wanting to cry for I know not how to do this
she says you cannot but speak now
for there is sight
the magic is gone.

I see for the first time I see.
I laugh and she laughs
my soul grows strong and tall.
I am quickening as I see.
The Priestess asks me to speak of what is seen
I flinch and realize that the fear has gone.
Speaking to her and myself of what I have seen.

And I said:
I am the justice of the world
bringing both life and balance to the seasons.
Acceptance of life is a judgment of being fully formed.
I choose to judge life as good and fully formed.

I am the ears of the world.
For I alone can hear the quickening of my soul.
I hear the music of my body
and the universe and know they are one.
I hear the pain and the hurt
and know they are from using
magic and not love.
I choose to hear only the Truth
as the Priestess tells me it is so.

I choose not to judge Truth as good or bad
or as anything other than life and love.
I choose to only hear Truth in all life.
In this choice I have given myself a body of light
and love that is for an eternity of peace.
A fertile body that will bring forth life in love,
justice and knowingness to all who come to the Priestess.
A body that will continue through all time
to purify itself through the ritual of earth, water and fire
taking itself to the breath of life
that it may have consciousness.

I have chosen my voice.
It will be one of Sight.
Gentle, loving, and fully formed.
In the gentleness and acceptance
of the seeds of consciousness it
finds the strength of all times.
For it will speak only the Truth
in its speech it will bring forth the Truth in all that hear.
This is the voice I share with the Priestess.
In this acceptance I AM I
the divinity is accepted
will speak to all who would hear.

Before all this is the word.
The word is the Sight
I choose this sight as fully formed
this voice as fully formed for all times.
I have chosen my eyes and they are fully formed.
For they have seen Truth
in all that is brought forth
they will see justice and knowing
God is good
the divinity is always seen in all.
Fully formed known in all life
there must be a ritual of earth, water, fire
finally consciousness becomes the breath of life.

My eyes will see this for all who come to me.
The Priestess and I will share this for an eternity
Seeing both backward and forward
beyond all time and space.
The clarity of sight is
the sight of the divine knowing all that is now.

I have chosen my heart
it is a heart filled with compassion and love.
In its compassion embraces the Truth in all that hurt.
Laughing at their magic and fear of the trolls.
laughing through out eternity for the joy of it all.

Embracing the weary
My heart beating for them while they die.
It is fully formed.
Filled with thought for all thought
filled with compassion, love
knowing this for an eternity.
Knowing this is the Truth for all who come.

Beating to sustain all life
Hope, joy and laughter as Truth
it is fully formed and beating now.

I have chosen my arms.
They are soft and long
fully formed for they embrace the
Truth for an eternity.
Never growing weary of the timelessness of Truth
Nor do they feel the weight of the world
they are the Truth
holding not magic or fear in their embrace.
fully formed and holding all who come in timeless Truth.

I have Chosen my feet.
soft and knowing
they walk upon the new earth I am choosing.
Strong and fully formed walking
throughout eternity without growing weary
understanding of Truth in infinite manifestation.
Knowing all there is, is Truth
beside this there is nothing else.
In their knowing they will walk a path,
which will allow others to follow.

They will know the jungle, mountain, ocean and meadows
knowing all paths lead to the Truth.
Each path shall be known as divine destiny.
Fully formed feet tell the voice to give
instructions on the path
the ears will know
the heart will beat
this fully formed body knows itself as divine,
pure in thought and fully formed as Truth.

I have chosen my mind
it is one of sight and knowing.
Fully formed, of pure thought
for it is the breath of life
consciousness.
Listening to the sight and knowing of Truth.
Knowing all life is consciousness,
purpose and destiny of mind
to know all life as consciousness.
It gives this to the voice to speak
to all those who hear.
Fulfillment and peace of purpose are found.

I have chosen my lips
they are fully formed
are seen and full for they form the words for the voice.
Speaking only the Truth
kissing only as Truth for there is nothing else to kiss.
All understand the words
for they form the words of Truth
touching the soul of all who come.
In their speech caressing the fully formed body of Truth

I have chosen my passion and fire.
It is the fire of the seasons
the fire of Truth for there is no other fire or passion.
This passion and fire burn all the magic and trolls.
Bringing forth the sun and light in all life.
It always has been and is for an eternity.

Knowing life being fed by the air of consciousness
to bring forth greater and greater love and Truth
releasing it into our lives
Heating the earth so it may bring forth
an abundance of life

warming waters so they may nourish and purify
the soul upon the path of Truth
burning without pain and hurt
bringing me to the peak of my mountain
where I see clearly and know only Truth.
I have chosen to feel all life.
Choosing to have fully formed sensual abilities.
Life must feel to know Truth
in this sensualness there is only the Truth.
Knowing how all life feels
the feelings of Truth
feeling as mind as consciousness
there is nothing else to feel but this.
In this sensualness I call upon my passion
to take me to my peak
to know me as Truth as the one beingness.
My sensualness will tell my voice to speak
of this to all those who will hear.

I have chosen my sexuality today.
Choosing to be fully formed as a gift of life.
It is the way in which Truth manifest
using passion and sensualness
to bring forth life in all that is a fully formed being.
In my sexuality I have accepted myself as one
this is the Priestess this one being.
known as one being this day as fully formed
Truth knowing itself as Truth,
Manifesting as the Priestess of Melchizedek.
the Priestess shall see all of this is heard
by those who would hear.
She accepts the divine knowing;
as the judge and the knower of all life.

The Priestess embraces me for the first time
for now I am fully formed
we laugh and love
for there is nothing else but Divine Truth.

In all of this a new heaven and earth have been formed
so we might know this as our path
in our knowing of Truth.
Truth Knowing Itself As Truth As Consciousness.
In this day I have chosen to be a woman
fully formed as Truth
giving birth to myself as love and acceptance of love.
In this act of birth acceptance
of my fully formed being of Truth,
Accepting all my power as beingness
for now and evermore
And as it is written so it shall be thorough out eternity as
the word.

May 1998

Desire

Standing on the edge of my universe
Finding the cliff of insanity,
toes wiggling over the edge in anticipation.

Swirls of clouds and stars appear
then drift out of sight.
Winds of light sweep pass
churning the atmosphere into a hectic energy.

Being is pulsating to unknown
rhythms of creative forces.
Each new vision brings me closer
to the reality I am.

Slowly my hand reaches out
touching the softness of life itself
the shock of new life energy travels through senses
exploding in my mind like a cascade
of eternal experiences.

I am I and none other.
I am this life only witnessed.
I am I in an exquisite moment of desire.

Once more I reach out to touch
again finding desire
and experience of being.
I am I.
Slowly turning to see

Being surrounded by the turbulent winds
of light beckoning
me to a new place in life.

The desire of being wells up
wanting to know I am I.
This desire is strong,
driving me closer
to the edge of the cliff,
the cliff that feels like insanity.

The fear of what will be
comes to my throat,
wanting to step over the edge
but I cannot speak of this fear.
All reason has left my thoughts
all barriers have been surrendered
pulsating heart will not let this rest.

This long journey must be completed
to be whole and perfect in expression of being.
More than anything this is desired.
Thirsting for this experience
that strips all will and ego.

Yet I cannot tell you what it is.
It cannot be described
It is that which has no description.
I can only speak of what surrounds
me in this moment of encounter.

The desire to know to be I am I
comes forth again pushing
me once more to the brink of chaos,

This must be insanity.
There is no other way,
stepping over the edge of all reason,
surrendering life for this greater pull on being.
Looking below there is great chaos,
Indescribable visions
sights never before seen,
sounds never before heard.
The fluidity of life surrounds me
leaving me without form
or stars to guide this journey.

The winds of light have
pushed me over the edge
into the pit of insanity
my throat cannot scream its fear
nor my heart stop itself from pounding.
The desire to know what is ahead
pushes me deeper into this moment of chaos.
At last surrender
to this that will be in my life.

Being cannot comprehend
what is to be it can only accept
this moment of light and vision
in the moment of surrender
Accepting that which has always been.

I am I.

I am I is known
in this moment of desire and surrender
desire has created a new reality of consciousness
consciousness aware of consciousness.

The sounds are the songs of life itself
of the reality created
in this moment of desire and surrender.
Insanity has turned into order and reason
this is life,
this is my life as consciousness.
Filled with sounds of life and love,
with understanding
the reality I am I,
I am the creator of my reality,
I am the creator of my awareness.

Out of my desire comes consciousness
aware of itself as consciousness
the reality of being. I am I.
As I desire so shall I create.

October 22, 2007

Creativity

Chaos everywhere
pulling me from my thoughts,
Chaos everywhere leaving no room
for the order so sought...

Chaos and imbalance
touch every possession
wanting to toss them to a great unknown.
Chaos unrelenting
will not leave my consciousness,
haunting me beyond all time and space.

The simplistic order of a younger,
less experienced time is swept from me...
destroyed in the growing pandemonium.
No stepping back to grasp at an earlier principle.
No handrails for safety
new path appears
taking me deeper
into the disorganized swirl of creativity.

Turmoil and disorder
Thundering in my head,
pulling at my consciousness
as the door at the top begins to open.
Thundering footsteps of my father
haunt my last efforts to withdraw.

Pulls of past eclipses upon my sight.
Sweat upon my brow for the efforts unspent.
Elusive for all time,
order and perfection cannot be mine.

Heat rising in my throat
steps are mounted one at a time.
Blinding light from the open door,
thundering sounds that will not be.

Chaos seeking principle
clashes upon the night.
Heat in my body from
the effort now spent.
Heat in my soul
for this door leads to the fires of all times.

Heat rising beyond all conception...
beyond the chaos and confusion.
swirling, dancing in inextricable rhythms
only the soul can hear.

Chaos that will not know perfection
has been loosed upon my world.
Stepping upon the top step,
it is known,
fully known that this will end
all that has been conceived.
the fires that will not stop.

Consumed by the fires
the life that was born.
As the last ash is flung
chaos is experienced for all time.

Unending aberration that will not cease.
Vital chaos is lifeforce unfolding.
Freed at last from the constraint of order,
loosed upon the wind as ash in the sky.

Creative urge to haunt all that was known.
Freed at last to dance the rhythm of all time.
Vital is the chaos for the seeds of life are there.
The moment of conception has no law or course to take.
Only Chaos unfolding to know itself as life.

April 23, 2000

Beyond Hope

Beyond all hope I have seen
and heard
the song remains weak,
But in the lyric and tone is hope

Beyond all hope I have felt
Trusting what is known
The vibration of love feels weak
in the waves of warmth of being is hope

Beyond all hope I have found this day
finding existence in my trust
The words are soft and different
but in this sound truth is found.

Beyond all hope I have found divinity
In my trust all that is to be is present
This knowing is in itself is grace
In this moment we stand in grace.

Beyond all hope I have seen God in your face
Reaching for that which is your being
Touching your being and mine
in this moment is eternity for we are one spirit as love.

I have seen our spirit
known our grace
experienced our love
singing our song
dancing our dance

October 27, 2007

Think left and think right and think low and think high.
Oh, the thinks you can think up if only you try!

~Dr. Seuss, Oh, the Thinks You Can Think!

Giving chocolate to others is an intimate form of communication, a sharing of deep, dark secrets

Milton Zelman, publisher of "Chocolate News"

Flights of Fantasy

Love without fantasy is like a star without a moon... they go together, they belong together. When we fall in love we fall into fantasy, and if we try we might keep that fantasy for a lifetime. Each of our relationships is hidden behind a mysterious cloud, a mask we wear... roles we play...

Day-by-day, night-by-night we carve out the angel we have come to love... revealing what is behind the mask, we pull it from our lover's face, they pull it from ours to reveal the final fantasies... to reveal the underlying world we have built. Perhaps the trick is to never let the fantasy become a reality. Instead to toy with it as we would a kitten and a string...pulling and moving erratically so no reality has a chance to set in...

What good is it if we catch a fairy and lock her up? The butterfly soon dies when we bind it away... love is like this it must remain in the world of fantasy... free to flit .. free to be. It is only what we fantasize that takes on life... what we imagine is the reality most of us live in.

What good is data, research if presented in a tedious manner? If we can't imagine our life filled with love and longing... then we will live in a dull grey world.

The garden of love is filled with fairies, butterflies, and yourown gossamer wings you have but to look for them. In my world of love, stars shine, moon beams play upon my pillows, fairies come and I fly with my wings.
May your life be filled with all that you dream.

Dreams

This morning fog fills my world
It covers the trees and gardens
This sweet mist softens all that it touches
My dream makes me want to stay asleep

The sweet mist makes me soft and surrendering
Is it my pillow that calls me or a deeper need
A dream of gender and trying to understand
A dream of luxury and fall leaves

Swirling leaves and scents fill my head
We sit and eat and I understand
My androgen is not what I thought it was
In this moment it could have been lost

It seemed to be hard and uncaring in my mind
This sweet mist has left me knowing
Soft and surrendering to a new kind of love

My being has been remade out of this love
Swirling mist taken me to new experiences of being
My androgen has returned soft and in surrender
A greater will and experience is known
The beloved waits my entrance

Into the consciousness of all times must I step

For Alice
October 31, 2007

The Fall

For a month I have watched you through my window
The leaves from the pear tree have fallen
Leaving only a few pears clinging to life
As you remain steady in my vision

When I see you the rainbow appears
Your being is so impressive
Tenacious in your work
Unmoved by the fall winds that rise

The bamboo faces the fall
As does the eucalyptus by just being
But you face the fall by working
I see you out my window

I have grown to love you from afar
Did you know I could love one like yourself?
You have given me sight about the fall
Did you know I am like you?

Spider dear spider will you sit and talk to me?
Tell me of your life
Give me the secret of the rainbow you weave
Help me prepare for the fall

Spider, dear spider invite me to your web

for Arachne
November 11, 2007

Only In The Spaces

Only in the spaces do I find you.
Your wrapper hidden behind
In the spaces I find no time
Looking for the meaning

In the spaces between
Nothing knowing nothing
Nothing experiencing nothing
No existence No meaning

Turning slowly to see what will not be seen
Slowly knowing that which has no meaning
I rolled over onto my back on our bed
on the ceiling is a spider

Never noticed how much went unnoticed
Soft light filters through our window
falling gently on the dust on the floor
I suppose I should get up and dust.

Darkness and numbness fill my head today
Failing to notice what we don't notice
we haven't, can't, won't change
we must see what we don't see,
looking in the spaces to find us

Wrappers bumping wrappers
Flesh against flesh
Finding no time
No meaning in the space between

Looking in the spaces to find us
Trying to see what we didn't see
Can't change us until we see
what would not be seen
Looking at the edge of the wrappers
What formed the edges?

Failing to notice the spaces
we did not know existed.
Turning on my side
kitchen needs cleaning
I suppose I should do the dishes.

December 3, 2007

On The Day You Were Born

On the day you were born
The stars shown upon the earth
The moon lit the path
And the velvet night waited

The ocean waves
rolled upon the sands
making a new path
birds sang and fish swam

On the day you were born
Flowers bloomed and
trees grew
fruit came to be

The lush green of the world
Pulsed
Knew
Became

On the day you were born
I knew purpose
Your name was in the stars
and written upon the sands

My hand reach beyond all time
to touch the softness of your skin
wanting to know the flow of your life
feeling the warmth of your heart.

On the day you were born
My heart took flight
eyes saw clearly as the world waited

I knew you would be with me
Waiting for you to walk the
silky path of life
see your stars in the sky
lay upon the sand the waves have kissed

On the day you were born
Life came to be
Love bloomed
and I had purpose.

for Eildon Gabriel
January 6, 2007

My Rabbit

Rabbit oh Rabbit you went down your hole
What shall I do while you're gone
Rabbit oh Rabbit may I come too

Rabbit oh Rabbit sitting on the hill
Silhouetted against the sky
Floppy ears and twitching whiskers
Dance against the sun

Rabbit oh Rabbit do not disappear
Shall I fix us tea?
Will you bring the crumpets?
Rabbit oh Rabbit do not disappear

Rabbit oh Rabbit the tea is ready
Shall we use the red Queen's cups?
The table is set and the crumpets laid
Rabbit oh Rabbit do not disappear

October 30, 2007

Touching

I turned to touch you and your face went away
I turned to reach you and found you not.
Turning, turning reaching to touch

Sad, so sad that I have not touched

I turned to see you and your face turned from me
I turned to reach you and you were not
Reaching, turning wanting to touch

Sad so sad that I have not touched

Turning to find the stars in your eyes
Turning to find the moon on your face
Reaching to find the beat of your heart

Wanting to touch, wanting to know
Turning to see what could have been missed
Turning to look for what will be
Reaching and finding softness

Touching, touching, touching

So happy so happy

October 15, 2007

Endless Time

It was an endless time
divorced from reality
a different kind of time

A time spent with someone
whose close proximity
brings sensual delight

Our bodies touch
shoulder, hip, thigh
knee and leg

Plunged forward in time
our flesh pressed against
flesh in tight embrace

A voyage that could
not last forever
but a time
we wish to savor

You told me of your hunger
And I gladly assuaged it
Curbing my own hunger
falling into a more luxurious state.

Storms once again gathering
winds of lust blowing around us
seas of desire lapping at our very existence

Finding safe haven
caves in this sea of sexuality
we have created

Safety from the seas domination
rocking in our cradle of love
new experiences as we climb
our mountains of solitude

November 17, 2007

A Moment of Magic

In this moment of magic
I have turned to see you
The illusion I thought is no more
Take this illusion and do what you may

It is magic this morning
Slowly turning I see the moon in your eyes
Turning I feel your skin next to mine
Once more I turn and embrace the beauty you are

Joy in this moment of magic we have found
As you turn I see the sun on your face
Our feet have touched the velvet of the night sky
The stars will guide us to this moment of ecstasy we seek
All things are possible in this moment of magic

Reaching I pull you to me
Touching your face and shoulder
I smell the scent of love on you
Magic is everywhere now

We cannot escape this moment of love
I could have lost you in my turning from it
But instead I have found you
In all things are magic today

Turning I reach f your heart
That I may know the pulse of life you are
Turning I offer you my heart

Magic is there as I turn to see you once more
Turning I have known forever you in my life
You are the illusion I dreamt of, sought in my dreams
Turning so you may see my soul

Magic is in the very words you whisper to me
As you speak I turn to know your soul
I could have lost you in my turning
I will find you in this magic we are creating

Your magic has given me life today
The very touch of your hand on my body
Has created ecstasy through my being
Let this magic remain forever

My passion for you is not magic
There is no illusion about my need for you

February 1, 2008

I Could Write a Book

I should write about how I love you,
About the love in your eyes
The touch of your hand in mine

I could write about how your voice sounds
The touch of your words
makes me
shudder in pleasure

I could write about how I love you
How the stars glow brighter
when you come to me
and the air smells of spring

It would take a book
To tell you
all of the ways I love you
all the ways I want you

Would you read my book of love?
Will you see how I love you?
Look into the sky
and see the star created for you

Will you let me write about you?
I want to tell the world how I love you
I want to tell the world how
you have changed my very existence

The world should know
how the breezes whisper your name
The streams sigh when you pass
Birds wait to sing their songs for you

It will take a book
For the world to know
How much I love you

I could write for an eternity
Telling the world how you hold my hand
and touch me
taking me to your place of love…

December 7, 2007

Hold my hand
Touch me
Let me take you
To my place of love

The Twelve Ways of Christmas

My true love asked me what I wanted
My heart stood still and then I knew

On the 1st day of Christmas
Under the pear tree in the garden
do I want you...
Take me in the spring
when the blossoms bloom

On the 2nd Day of Christmas
Soft cooing and kisses
To start my day
The dove of love
Keep it close to me

On the 3rd day of Christmas
Deep French kisses
Soft velvet lips on mine
Electricity in my mind
Kissing for an eternity

On the 4th day of Christmas
Speak to me of love,
Tell me the ways
You will love me and
take me in your passion

On the 5th day of Christmas
Tell me how we will
Love forever
Give me your
Promise of desire unending

On the 6th day of Christmas
Let my heart take wing
That the fervor and love
shall set us free

On the 7th Day of Christmas
The water of life is in our love
Let me smell you
Taste your love
and drink of our creation

On The 8th Day of Christmas
Find me in our bed
Take me without reservation
I want all of you

On The 9th Day of Christmas
Dance naked with me in our garden
Wind blows its velvet touch as
flesh meets flesh
Fulfill the hunger for the fruit we grow

On The 10th Day of Christmas
Stand with me in our shower
Lay with me in our tub
Play with me in the pool of delight
Be forever in the sea of sexuality

On the 11th Day of Christmas
Sing to me o love
Speak to me of your carnal desire
Take me to my fantasy with your words
Penetrate my very being with meaning

On The 12th Day of Christmas
My head is pounding with torment
Body throbbing in its wanting
Feeling you devour my being
Taking me to new places of fulfillment

Singing the hallelujah Chorus

December 17, 2007

Billows of Steam

Billows of steam from the shower
Water droplets on my skin
Gradually wash away the scents of our love

Soap and love flowing into the drain of nowhere
Water on my face hides the tears
Steam carrying the memory of us

My prayer unanswered for one more night
Hopes burst like the bubbles of my shampoo
How can this happen

So many days and plans thrown away
Steam covers my mirror
I don't want to face what I will see

You have gone to fantasy
Billows of steam from the shower
Hiding the cloudiness of thought

Covering the dawning of love
Drops of love
Upon the bed are all that is left

Music on the wind begins to fade
Life passes
Day ends
I begin again

November 19, 2007

Secret Love

For ten years I have waited
for you to come to me.
We talked and shared
my fires of desire
never revealed to you
only dreamt and fantasized
about being your lover.
I wrapped my self in cotton
so you could never feel me.

Never in all my times with you,
did I allow my self to
touch the beauty of your being.
Not once did I bring your name
to my lips in moments of passion.

Locked away in my heart
I kept you secret from the world I lived.
At night I have laid in my bed
being loved by another.
Afraid my tears would reveal
my hidden secret of you.

Not once in all of these years
have I been free of you
and my love for you.
In all of these years
have you ever felt my love for you?

Did you know I existed?
When I came back to talk to you again,
did you know why?
Give me a crumb something to hope for.
For one moment let me be in your arms.

Night after night I am tormented
in my wanting of you.
I keep you hidden away in my heart
where no one can find you.
Tossing and turning in my dreams
reaching through the passage we created years ago.

Dreaming your fingers reach me, touching
me gently opening my being to yours.
How real is this fantasy.
Desiring simple things,
holding your hand,
fixing food
working in our garden.

I see the breeze blow the curtains,
tossed sheets, burnt candles.
Wanting the simple things to share with you.

Once again we are talking and laughing.
Of things others would find silly
or of little use in the building of life.

Are your fingers the same as the dream?
Looking in our talk for our common ground.
Is there enough to build upon?

Now we are sharing our life ideas.
I am having hope once again
that you will find your way to my bed
to my arms where I may love you,
simple things like fixing you a favorite food.
Making sure life is comfortable for you.

Nothing can be altered,
no change of heart
no place I can hide from this and us.
The secret will be known.
Is this an experiment of God in trust?

Suddenly you are in
my every word and thought.
You have said you will come.
You will share my bed and
life for a few short days.

Is this what it will be?
We have begun to share small things,
a poem, a gift, a plant.
Wanting you so much I can't breathe.

Heart beating loudly
I can barely utter your name.
I am sure you are all over my face.
Come quickly before I suffocate
in my desire for you and my secret is known.

December 20, 2007

Soft Light

I woke to soft light
Smells of your being
in my bed
fingers reaching to find you

Every morning for a week
You have been the first
thought on my mind
blocking all other

Faires come and whisper to me
your name and life
let me have my wings
that I might fly to find you

April 2, 2008

Lady of The Lake

And I stood with my feet in the lake...
water lapping at my feet
coolness penetrating the heat of my Beltane fires.
looking upward
moon descended onto me filling me
with radiance on the darkest of nights..

Swirling in me
my being raising my love
higher and higher into the universe
lifeforce throbbing in my head
heart pulsating to a new rhythm…
swirling leaving none of me in the same spot

When I thought I was lost
the earth rose up to meet me
and embrace me
taking me to the depths of my fire
burning deep cold burning
beyond all time and space

Knowing in a different way…
And my body moved in a new way
to the rhythms of the earth
and moon
lifting me up into a new state of being
flowing out and back as love
reaching and staying
going and coming all at once

I am I the one beingness
the music of it all... earth and moon
singing their chorus of hallelujah ...
I Am the I Am
and now I Am the Ava Maria
knowing forever the rhythm of love.

Behold the Lady as she rises out of me
touching the moon
taking the earth to her breast to nourish
and feed it so that it might bring forth in love

My spirit has new understanding new sight
Going beyond the Lady and the King
no more sky or stars or moon or earth
no more me no more to be.

I knew not more as me
only as the rhythm of Truth and love
One beinginess without beginning or end
the earth and heavens
were born again as one
and so it is written and so it shall be.

November 11, 2000

Silent Crossing

Silently the shadow crosses my wall,
lingering, holding… being.
Silently the shadow crosses my path
Floating not walking
being not knowing
just being

Silently floating into the mist,
rolling, tumbling mist covers my beloved trees,
fills them with jewel like crystals.
Rolling and tumbling across my path as
I float on the mountains of dew.

Touching each small crystal with my sight.
Silently floating the shadow crosses my path.
The Silence deepens as
I float to the lake, tumbling upon the mist,
rolling with the breeze.

The shadow crosses my path
how many times will it cross?
How long will it linger with me?
Silently holding,
being not knowing,
crossing my path.

Just being in silence.
Dancing swirling in the mist,
covered in crystals of light..

Silent crossing.
Tumbling with the mist
Shadow upon the mist.
Floating on the breeze.

Reaching this shadow
that has crossed my path
many times in silence,
reaching through the mist,
as we tumble, rolling not knowing just being,
touching in the silence

Reaching mist as the
shadow swirls and dances upon the dew
covered in crystals of light.
Dancing, swirling, lingering, holding.
Silence in my mind,
song in my throat.
Reaching to touch the shadow.

Glowing as the dew,
rolling as the breeze
silent as the tree.
Holding the shadow
so it will be with me,
but it pulls and tumbles across my path.

Silent crossing.
Sparking as a crystal in the light
glowing as the dew.

Mist upon the beloved trees
glowing as the light upon the dew
sparking as the crystal in the light..
Touching the tree
and the dew.

Touching the mist with my mind
wanting to be in the light.
Rising and falling upon the breeze

filled with the silence of mind
and the hallelujah of my song.

Mind filled with silence,
throat filled with song,
touching the mist

Light rising above the mist
silence in the mind
rising above the mist,
song in my throat
being with the shadow that crosses my path
silent crossing... mystical being.

Dancing, twirling and mixing
riding upon the light
holding the light
silence in the mind
Dancing in the stream of light
the silence.

Joyous being
silence of the mind,
joyous feeling I
holding in the joy of all time.

Joyous light of being.
creating for all time.
Life that has been
always will be.
Light that has been is for all time
being for all time
Joyous holding,

lingering,
being as silence of all mind
living being creating as light.

Dancing on the silence.
New life to be, always has been.
Dancing, lingering, being for all time
Joyous life that has been and always will be

for Tim
Spring 2001

I Don't Know You

I know nothing of you
Not knowing what kind of music you like
or scents of incense
or favorite movies
or books
or food.
what you really do on the weekend.

I do not know if you can match my intensity.
can match my passion
will trust me to take us to God.?

I do not know if you
like laying on the beach
flying a kite...
Is your favorite color the sun setting
or the blue of the lake
or green of new leaves.

Do you like the smell of sweat?
Do you like the feel of a soft animal curled up
purring or sighing beside you.
Do you drink tea and read in bed...
Do you burn candles and listen to the quiet...
to seek beyond the stars for the intent of all life.

I do not know you..
How am I to know you?
And for you .. how are you to know me?

Do not take me lightly or with
little profoundness..
for my life is full of many things
you have not discovered...
I have never let a lover go easily
binding them to our time and space
so that our companionship
will serve us well throughout eternity

We are bonding if you go
I will be sad in a rather ordinary
way of expressing myself.
in the end you will remain my friend
and lover for an eternity.

For you touched my soul
taking me to God
I have touched your soul
taking you to God
we have known each other
in knowledge and being

My irritations are little
have little do with you
but with the rhythm and
symbols that play out in our lives
waiting for the arriving time
and place for new cycles to begin

I am not an a gap that has holes to be filled
or self esteem to be built
or a god to be discovered
I have experienced God
standing beyond all time and space.

I am like Dante
returning from hell and mountain peak
knowing who I am
yet not knowing

Who are you in this scheme
laying itself before me?

I am I
I am Sophia,
Counselor most high,
Melchezidek,
I am I

Who are you?

February 25, 2000

Fog

Fog covering the trees
swirling over the ground
reaching for the sky
How am I to find you?

Fog covering the stones
laying on top of our music
covering the sky and the stars
How am I to find you?

Fog blocking the future
swirling in and out of consciousness
laying on the path to find you
Reach me through the fog
touch the path we walk on
let the fog roll back

Join me I am sitting on the moon waiting

October 25, 2007

When I Went To Bed

When I went to bed
you were there on my mind
I tossed and turned thinking of you

Imagined what it would be like
to have you beside me
touching me, wanting me

Through the night your image filled my dreams
Stormy love and passion
untold romps through my head

In my dreams I reach out to touch you
Dreaming of your touch and love on me
I want you in my bed this morning
I am filled with passion

And the need to love you
Rolling over on my back I wonder
How will you fit into my life
What if you leave me?

Come to me in my dream
Or in my day time
But come and be with me
Let me know and love you

How am I to survive this passion I feel for you?

November 23, 2007

She is a friend of mind. She gather me, man. The pieces I am, she gather them and give them back to me in all the right order. It's good, you know, when you got a woman who is a friend of your mind.

~Toni Morrison, Beloved

There's nothing better than a good friend, except a good friend with CHOCOLATE

~Linda Grayson, "The Pickwick Papers"

Friends and Lovers

In many ways friends are as important and sometimes more important than lovers. And yet would I be as I am without lovers? Can we really tell the difference between a lover and a friend?

I watch my family, brother and father, and see that they may have started as lovers with their mates... but now, after many years, they are lovers and friends, caring for each other...filled with compassion and wisdom almost as if the two hearts beat as one.

My soul needs no other to be complete, but my consciousness longs for others to share... food, gardens, poetry, and moments of love. This I believe is what friends do... they share ... giving to one another, embracing each other in our journey and imparting wisdom gained from experience... These poems came from friends... from lovers... from hearts that wanted to share and be accepted. I could not have asked for a more sacred gift than being allowed to include these in this work of love.

July 29, 2008
West Linn, Oregon

Wisp

I catch a mid-summer bus
at a non-descript grid point,
like any across a vast territory.

The rear of the bus a seat
and window fulfills desire,
my ever grinding need for isolation.

Lumbering past suburbs,
a father is mowing lawn,
his young daughter runs gleefully before him.

She, dressed in sharp blue quickened,
her long blonde hair whirled, tousled,
the image of a tiny aeonian.

She has run to pick blossoms,
gray and seeded dandelions,
viewing the dry crowns with curious blue eyes.

One puff issued from small lips,
a cordate rubicund mouth
scatters cognizant sentience to azure.

one, remains before her gaze,
her countenance is as though
the seed were a resplendent mystical thing.

In the moment it takes light
to fly across an angstrom,
that picture is shot firm within my mind.

with closed eyes I follow that
minute, seamless, diadem
into cobalt deep and darkened transcendence.

Drifting over this above that,
mountains of black affliction,
diving into places within nothingness.

moving towards the distant clouds,
brash achromic dissonance,
fluttering like sheets blown about in the wind.

In my waking awareness
the diadem now missing
dark becomes light as I ask "where are you wisp?"

P.M.H
January 22, 2008

Have You

we knew love once - when love burnt my eyes so
i may fall face first onto day and night and
lives of stabbing emotions and affairs
of a very human nature

i knew you once - that day we stopped to rest
and noticed a spot of blood where
some newly born thorn pricked your skin

we knew that red day tears and pain
and felt love in flesh and died and
grew though in our minds fell dumb again

only nothing soft touched my face that afternoon
after i spoke your name and
knew the sticky red taste of love
slowly dripping from that well
you held for me - so rightly

today, this morning, the soft illusions of dreams
and youth lie discarded and
what beauty wrought beauty decays

and i ask you have you felt love

have you seen beauty

 i ask you to spare nothing as i spare very little –
and in this i find beauty and love mean the world to me –

we felt loss that day
so again i ask you what does love feel like?

how far into depravity does love abide?
and i wonder why beauty bleeds such filth

how can we see both night and day clearly
and love each equally –
ask each to pass our lips and savor bitter and sweet

i feel you passing by my lips - the soft form of words,
born from one tear that fell from you through me onto
this
page
and i smile
for i know you love me still

Greg Fiendell
July 14, 2008

Crystalization

I walk out, down the doorstep,
into the thick woods that
conceal the neatly rowed,
preened, rectangular boxes
of dwelling.

Shapes that shatter the spherical
mandala of consciousness into shards
of disjointed, irregular, relative
truth.

On my way in I pass patches of scattered
mushroom fairy rings. I want to touch them
but pull away for fear that my curiosity
may destroy the magical and circular
beauty of them.

still the vision of that doorstep remains
crystal and fixed upon my mind.
At the center of the tangled overgrown
woods is a body of water, a lagoon
with an oriental style bridge that
crosses at one end of it.

The lagoon once a limb of an oxbow
river now severed and a member of
this isolated place.

I step precariously upon it and peer
over the railing. my reflection takes
the form of a fun house mirror, but
the joy of it is lost to me.
Blue sapphire settings drift overhead

showering splinters of glass upon the
rolling naked water. Needle sharp,
piercing little spirits that play
in the heart and mind.

Reflecting, Had I only invited the
vision of that doorstep in.

Outside the wooded ring there is a halo.
The glow of streetlamps give the illusion
that I've crossed into some timeless and
ancient place.

Time to go back. On the way out I stop to
look upon the rings and wildflower blossoms
shrouded in the cool blanket of night.
Giant trees reach out to me in their
empathy, they are old wizards waiting
for a time to awaken.

the cobblestone streets, concrete, glass
and luminosity, bear the resemblance of
an old world village. The time and manner
of civil reciprocities long forgotten.

Me, without my glasses have a Renoir view of it.
Home now, my foot resting upon the doorstep,
pausing before going in.
I remember Crystal,
loved her dark eyes.
she sat on my doorstep,
running a finger
through a hole   *P. M. H.*
in the leg of her jeans.   *2007*

Desire

I am I within and surronding
I am not experiences it's universe of contact.
To touch, to seek,
driving me madly to the edge of myself
of all that I am not..
Vistas of what might be, appear and disappear,
within, and without,
perceived through the wrapper of
twisting and swirling glass convulting, convulsing.

I am I -
oh so that might touch to enfold that I am
NOT that I am I those I am I(s).
I know only what is between -
I only infer - I am I is surrounded by the experience
of what I am Not enfolding, enfolded.
Rolling, turning, with each grasp of breathe,
of being, I breath in and out so I might know,
purely, simply, to know that which I do not know.

Yet each time as I turn,
breathe, I only feel more of I am I,
enfolded by I am not,
enfolding I am Not enfolded I am I.
It's breath blowing me to what I do not know, can not
know, want to know.
I can almost smell it, my nose, turning towards.
I must find this, I am I seeking, thirsting, breathing,
driving, wishing, softly, turning.

I am I am enfolding together, All I am, crazy seeking, ter-
rifyingly NOT, enfolding one act contact,
desire
know I enfolding enfolded
infolding..

I am I am lost, falling, freely into that I am NOT
enfolded,
enfolding I am I breathing, beating, pulsing, wholly,
together, touching, knowing.

All I am, all I know is this insanity, this maddeningly
crazy seeking, itching, aching, sucking, enfolding, turning,
terrifyingly terrific adventuring into the uncontrollable
NOT, enfolding I am, contact, exploring.. I am this, this
one act of creation ISness, Now, this moment.
contact,
desire
know I am NOT
enfolding I am I
enfolded
infolding.

RJR
October 22, 2007
R in response to S Desire..

This is the Lesson on Crossing the Sands.

Remember it.
The sands are wide,
the oases few.
It is always safest to remain where
you are.

But if you cannot
remain where you are,
then it is safest to go with a caravan.

But if there is no caravan, then it is safest to go with a
trusted band of companions.

But if there are no trusted companions,
then it is safest to go with one
who knows the sands.

But if there is no one who knows the sands,
then you must cross the sands alone.
There are two things to remember.

First, take nothing with you but what sustains you:
food and water. If you cannot take both,
leave the food but carry the water.
You must carry the water if you are to cross the sands.

Second, never attempt to travel by daylight:
the sun will kill you.

You must wait until nightfall; then it will be safe to travel.
Moonlight and darkness will be light enough.

There are two things you must do. Stay alive.
And keep moving. If
you can do just those two things,
you will come to another oasis.

This is the Lesson on Crossing the Sands. Remember it.

M. R. Ritley
March 24, 2005

*note: MR was a wonderful writer she passed this year... this is a Sufi
lesson on the journey we each must take... it is symbolic of the long
night where we search our soul and go into the unconscious mind.*

I Am Undone

when i rest do the songs i sing remind you of me
when you listen can you hear me, calling
how can i wake without you
or do i choose another amusing heartache
or am i such a villain to deserve this absence
or, more rightly, am i so self absorbed
to presume some stature at your feet
so close as to remain blind
your voice ineffable to my vulgar ears

if struck so dumb why do i ache so
why know so much and arrive so late
dear Muse may i demand of you,
Love me in Song, Love me awake,
Love me asleep, Love me - or do you?

you must - love me
my heart cries out and you love
dare i ask for your hand
a touch of which might tangle my world with yours
i would sip of poison leaf for a moment of Grace
to realise your Name and clear the web from my eyes

in the end i am only undone, in love
laid naked for all to view
what will you tell me when my last
mask falls away to reveal my worth,
the last drops of life caught on a
canvas of our making

a chord struck on every second of my life
ever in accordance to a fancy of my making
will the sound of my life assualt your exquiste nature?
will you smile?

if asked would you fly without question
into an air of uncertainty
into pain and joy in equal parts
where do we fly where every horizon dawns without dusk
in this absence do we then know longing and desire
can a heart ever exist in love without doubt
or a dawn without dusk

perhaps, in some dream, a lover will remain
in friendship a morning will turn dusk into day
day into night - and night into flight
into the night our Dragon will fly
and on into day the dreams of two lovers will echo
one off the other
only fading from those who remain - still

if ever i needed to comfort of words
this day like the past 60 are wanting of words
so dear muse...where do you sleep
and in who's arms are you kept

Harlot! spreading your favour,
courting the very page i leave blank
i left blank for you -
the ink drying on my fingers while you
stain another's well - soiled with your beauty

i am here - deemed unclean - unkempt and unworthy -
left picking at the edges of a work drawn too near the fire
-too far from water to save -
but for a single line do i forget you -
a single word otherwise obscured by my tears
and your fleeting heart...

Love
so we fly
fly from dawn - settle at night -
lovers favour darkness - words favour light -
so my muse walk with me a little further -
stain this page in dew -
hold my tired hand one night longer
and whisper in my ear of past longings,
of lovers passed over for another flight of fancy -
tell me of pain, of joy,
of great galleons brimming with stolen gold,
two days from freedom,
only to find Fate on the wind and death on a reef -
what stories will you whisper as a rest -
whose ear your breathe to reach -
whose heart your tears to touch

Greg Fiendell
November 1, 2006

I Want You

I have an idea that I want you.
My hands touch something, keys, stones,
pearls of your being.
Tapping out tones, syllables,
song like echos of 'hey', 'hi' what' up?

Somewhere deep inside there is something
I want to touch of you.
About what I think of you that I want.
A hunger insatible, desirable, unfufillable,
sucking in everything, consuming itself, renewing itself
this 'I want', with a renewed fury consuming
all logic and reason
with passionable want.

Today I breath you, wanting,
longing to feel the warmth of you
wanting that idea of you,
the warmth, smiling, welcoming.
Falling, swelling, growing, like a hunger for 'more'
this wanting that, wishing, longing, breath.
I whispered your name today, wanting you there, here,
everywhere, around me. I wrapped into your enfolded
grace, praying of us, of we, wanting you, us.

I
Want
you

RJR
November 17, 2007

Lion

It lies down the staircase
in the darkened basements.
There, pacing to and fro
like the liquid ocean.

In the broad light of day
dancing all about you.
Earth, water, fire and sky
sated in joyfullness.

Knocking upon your door,
void of your believing.
Biding you to come play,
within it's noone-ness.

Cat and mouse tournaments.
Always winning the chaff.
Omniscient lightspeed,
piercing through ignorance.

following you, crouching,
watching your busyness.
Invading privacy,
in every soft moment.

Melting around your bed,
in the swirling darkness.
Forms almost familiar,
daring you look within.

Calling out your namesake,
from the depths of dreaming.
Affronting security,
with faintly heard whisper.

"Come out of your temple,
that I may devour you.
That I may taste the warm,
sweetness of your surrender."

P.M.H
2008

At First

At first I was but only a spark,
an itch,
the scratch,
spurred piece of frictional rub.
With that first frame of motion I became,

I could feel my heat,
consuming everything consumable,
probing,
ripping apart with my mere presence the atoms of life,
burning myself brighter than the light
of billions of suns upon the cosmos.
I am Fire

Unbridled,
tearing,
exploding,
like a terrific flood consciousness consuming,
feeling, steering.
Driving.

I stabbed into the heart of space,
screaming,
my form,
calling into being,
force,
ordering the heart of chaos
making it mine,
rendering it self
subsuming
Empowering

Rippling across the vastness
the echo of the impulse
followed by a river of thought,
action,
doing
exploding into form
pulsating,
pumping,
growing,

turning the seeds of power
it's raw form evervescent
glowing, hot, raw heat

Focused,
intensified,
amplified,
engine of life,
at first rolling, then lifting and flying
and then rocketing faster, higher, into
this, that, you, me

Ohhh.. The roaring scream of being
filling the rocket engines of consciousness
lifting mountians upon suns of lofty ideals
or building weighty bridges
which span the chasms of realities.
These things and all greater I am.
For I
am
this
Purely singular
word   *RJR*
                                        November 19, 2007

Power

Kitchen Windows

From kitchen windows
view the world today.

Storms gather outside,
presage visages.

Run in for shelter
against the raging.

Things scattered about
like glyptics on scroll.

Cool, clear, forging rain drops fall changeling.
Thunder rolls against the mobius skies.
Augur wind screams though the trees and wire.
Extant disembodied voices wail.

So surreal paraph
upon blue-grey stele.

Drink toasts to this world
from taps hot and cold.

Of warm soothing love
or hot running hate.

P.M.H
2008

Silence

The silence is narcissistic,
We are wound deeply within it
.

Stillness, eternal Rubicon,
Venal desire of knowingness.

Chasing vaticinate riddles,
Maybe still yet yielding vision.

Interpretations are empty,
Leading to ignited conflicts.

Metamorphosis is in action,
Mindfulness of the discipline.

Evolutions survive inside,
Parallel yet running gantlets.

The white noise outside is rubble,
Vandalized ruins of confusion.

P.M.H
2007

Butterflies

Our love danced like butterflies,
landed on our lips, my smile, your kiss,
a joyous dance, a feel, intoxicating
as nectar can never be; we reeled and dipped
in flight far above our dancing heels.

Oh, my sweet love, when did it steal from us,
wander away in wornout skin shoes?
And how we tried to hold it, drug it back in bondage,
shod in heavy boots, with leaden toes and heels.
Anything to marry the magic to us.

Maybe it was seeing through the magic,
The slight of hand perceived, that broke the spell.
Or maybe, we had clung so long on the precipice
that we grasp acceptance and hung on
before resolve, too, fell beyond our reach.

We cannot endure this turmoil.
Tension, mounted to the breaking point,
waves collapsing in an angry ocean,
one followed by another, until the storm is spent
and momentary calm reigns.

What is there to free, flitting memories?
Modern tragedy, you say? Or meant?
No. Nor is it even an ancient rerun
from which we can absolve ourselves
the guilt and proclaim Fate undone us.

We are sinners to ourselves,
To the moral core of our hearts;
Our conscience, driving us into furies,
a rage that does not subside among the betrayed;
Those who once danced on delicate wings

Pat Kaes

Return to the Grotto

See, yonder young lovers, he straight, tall, proud;
her shining face, open, so vulnerable to him?
They walk in a meadow of their making, toward the
springs.
Soft the carpet of the meadow, soft their eyes,
Seeing with the heart, the mind eclipsed,
seeking the grotto, the immortal grotto, hidden, hidden.
Minne, goddess/tyrant of lovers, be kind to them.

Once we lay, two young lovers by Nigeria Springs,
misted by the watery crescendo;
the prisms of light fell onto the waters,
fell and we were lifted as on wings,
baptized in the cresting mixture,
wrapped in the fading sun and the song,
Do you remember the song, my darling,
ageless as Minne's grotto?

O, my Lover, is it enough, these dreams?
To cherish the butter cups of the meadow,
mingled with the purple thistles, fragrant,
sunny yellow, delicate soft purple blossoms
and the piercing thorns hidden in the leaves,
a bouquet of her liking, laid upon the altar
beside the double bladed sword.

From the fields the cows low at dusk,
coming to the sweet scented hay and I to you.
Husband's touch, warm, alive against my sagging flesh,
familiar in the declining light, draw me into that circle,
O, immortal circle, the coronal,
Like the matching rings on our hands,
or the bands around the departing moon.

The cows come for the honey-eyed oats,
For the exchange of gifts, like mine and yours,
Desires and needs craved of life's necessities like runes.
Lift us again to passions fed from on the crystalline bed,
forged in renewed memories -- Memories that run fleet-
ing,
cutting across the surface of our minds like killdeers,
the doleful, urgent calls of our hearts...and our immortal
love.

Pat Kaes

For The Love of Chocolate

When all is said and done I felt this work would not be finished unless we had a few more quotes on chocolate… and some recipes. Yummy… what could be better than spending time with your lover, love, partner, spouse, and having a healthy dose of chocolate.

I was allergic to chocolate and did not have my first taste until I was 6 years old. I remember the day better than I re-member my first day of school. I would take my chocolate at holidays and hide it. Savoring small pieces until the next holiday when more chocolate would appear. I still take a long time to eat my chocolate savouring each bite.

My mother often hid the chocolate as not to torment me, my keen sense of smell would find chocolate as soon as I stepped through the door. I could sniff it out anywhere. Later on my sons, Ethan and Andrew, could do the same. I will never forget their entrance into our home with "hey somebody has been eating chocolate."

Enjoy!

West Linn, Oregon
August 7, 2008

Strawberries and Chocolate

I like many kinds of fruits with chocolate, oranges, bananas, raspberries, blueberries, cherries and of course coffee beans. The right chocolate can be served with liquors and wines. I think some of the triple cream cheeses also lend themselves to being combined with good dark chocolate.

My favorite is strawberries and chocolate. I buy really good dark chocolate and melt it... dipping fresh strawberries into it. I let the chocolate cool and serve. You can do this samething with any fruit the suits your fancy.

Recipes Courtesy of Mary Spiers-Floyd

Fudge Brownies with Kahlua

1 1/2 c. sifted all purpose flour
1/2 tsp. baking powder
1/2 tsp. salt
2/3 c. butter
3 sqs. (1 oz. each) unsweetened chocolate
3 lg. eggs
2 c. granulated sugar
1/4 c. and 1 tbsp. kahlua
3/4 c. chopped walnuts or pecans

Grease 9 inch square pan well lined with foil. Preheat oven to 350 degrees. Resift flour with baking powder and salt. Melt butter with chocolate over low heat. Beat eggs with sugar until light. Add flour mixture, chocolate mixture and 1/4 cup kahlua blend well. Stir in nuts.

Turn into prepared pan. Bake 30 minutes or until top springs back when touched lightly in center and edges begin to pull away from pan. Remove oven cool thoroughly in pan. Brush top with 1 tablespoon kahlua. Cut into 1 x 2 inch bars. Makes 2 dozen.251

DoublerChocolate Chip Cookies

1 (6 oz.) pkg. semi-sweet chocolate chips, divided
1 1/2 c. all-purpose flour
1 tsp. baking powder
1/2 tsp. salt
1/2 c. shortening
1/2 c. sugar
1/2 c. packed brown sugar
1 egg
1 tsp. vanilla or orange extract
2 tbsp. milk
1 c. chopped walnuts (optional)
Place 1/2 cup chocolate chips in top of a double boiler.
Bring water to a boil. Reduce heat to low; cook until choco-
late melts, stirring occasionally. Cool. Combine flour, bak-
ing powder, and salt; set aside. Cream shortening; gradually
add sugars, beating well at medium speed.

Add melted chocolate, egg, and vanilla; beat well.
Stir in milk. Gradually add flour mixture and mix well.
Stir in remaining 1/2 cup chocolate chips and optional
walnuts.

Drop dough by heaping teaspoonfuls
onto lightly greased cookie sheets.
Bake at 350 degrees for 10 to 12 minutes.
About 6 dozen.

Colophon

Set in Garamond

using Adobe In design

This edition digitally printed
Portland, Oregon

www.onespiritpress.com
www.doublechocolate-exoticlove.com

www.ingramcontent.com/pod-product-compliance
Lightning Source LLC
Chambersburg PA
CBHW021049090426
42738CB00006B/251